COORDINATING SERVICES
FOR INCLUDED CHILDREN

INCLUSIVE EDUCATION

Series Editors:

Gary Thomas, Professor Education, Oxford Brookes University, and Christine O'Hanlon, School of Education, University of East Anglia

The movement towards inclusive education is gathering momentum throughout the world. But how is it realized in practice? The volumes within this series will examine the arguments for inclusive schools and the evidence for the success of inclusion. The intention behind the series is to fuse a discussion about the ideals behind inclusion with pictures of inclusion in practice. The aim is to straddle the theory/practice divide, keeping in mind the strong social and political principles behind the move to inclusion whilst observing and noting the practical challenges to be met.

Current and forthcoming titles:

Shereen Benjamin: *The Micropolitics of Inclusive Education*
Christine O'Hanlon: *Teacher Action Research for Social Inclusion*
Caroline Roaf: *Coordinating Services for Included Children*
Gary Thomas and Andrew Loxley: *Deconstructing Special Education and Constructing Inclusion*
Gary Thomas and Mark Vaughan: *Inclusive Education – A Reader*
Carol Vincent: *Including Parents?*

COORDINATING SERVICES FOR INCLUDED CHILDREN

Joined up action

Caroline Roaf

Open University Press
Buckingham · Philadelphia

Open University Press
Celtic Court
22 Ballmoor
Buckingham
MK18 1XW

email: enquiries@openup.co.uk
world wide web: www.openup.co.uk

and
325 Chestnut Street
Philadelphia, PA 19106, USA

First Published 2002

A catalogue record of this book is available from the Britisn Library

ISBN   0 335 21044 9 (pb)   0 335 21045 7 (hb)

Library of Congress Cataloging-in-Publication Data
Roaf, Caroline.
    Coordinating services for included children : joined up action / Caroline Roaf.
      p. cm. – (Inclusive education)
    Includes bibliographical references and index.
    ISBN 0-335-21045-7 – ISBN 0-335-21044-9 (pbk.)
    1. Children with social disabilities – Services for – Great Britain. 2. Youth with social disabilities – Services for – Great Britain. 3. Inclusive education.
    I. Title. II. Series.

HV751.A6 R63 2002
362.7′0941–dc21   2002023857

Typeset by Graphicraft Limited, Hong Kong
Printed in Great Britain by St Edmundsbury Press Limited,
Bury St Edmunds, Suffolk

Dedicated to the memory
of Patricia Vereker
who saw the potential of a new paradigm
and whose belief in the 'powerful influence'
of Networks remained undiminished.

Contents

Series editors' preface

'Inclusion' has become something of an international buzz-word. It is difficult to trace its provenance or the growth in its use over the last two decades, but what is certain is that it is now *de rigeur* for policy documents, mission statements and political speeches. It has become a slogan – almost obligatory in the discourse of all right-thinking people.

The problem about the sloganizing of 'inclusion' is that the word has become often merely a filler in the conversation. People can talk about 'inclusion' without really thinking about what they mean, merely to add a progressive gloss to what they are saying. Politicians who talk casually about the need for a more inclusive society know that they will be seen as open-minded and enlightened, and will be confident in the knowledge that all sorts of difficult practical questions can be circumvented. And if this happens, if there is insufficient thought about the nitty gritty mechanics, those who do work hard for inclusion can easily be dismissed as peddling empty promises.

This series is dedicated to examining in detail some of the ideas lying behind inclusive education. Inclusion, much more than 'integration' or 'mainstreaming', is embedded in a range of contexts – political and social as well as psychological and educational – and our aim in this series is to make some examination of these contexts. In providing a forum for discussion and critique we hope to help provide the basis for a wider intellectual and practical foundation for more inclusive practice in schools and elsewhere.

In noting that inclusive education is about more than simply 'integration', it is important to stress that inclusive education is really about extending the comprehensive ideal in education. Those who talk about it are therefore less concerned with children's supposed 'special educational needs' (and it is becoming increasingly difficult meaningfully to define what such needs are) and more concerned with developing an education system in which tolerance, diversity and equity are striven for. To aim for such developments is surely uncontentious; what is more controversial is the means by which this is done. There are many and varied ways of helping to develop more inclusive schools and the authors of this series look at some of these. While one focus in this has to be on the place and role of the special school, it is by no means the only focus: the thinking and practice which go on inside and outside schools may do much to exclude or marginalize children and the authors of this series try to give serious attention to such thinking and practice.

The books in this series therefore examine a range of matters: the knowledge of special education; the frames of analysis which have given legitimacy to such knowledge; the changing political mood which inspires a move to inclusion. In the context of all this, they also examine some new developments in inclusive thinking and practice inside and outside schools.

Caroline Roaf's book contributes to the debate about inclusion in a crucially important way. Recently, there has been much discussion about the ways in which we 'box up' services for children, with the boxes formed by professional, service and agency lines. Increasingly, it is realized that the firm lines of delineation drawn between one service and another may have unhelpful or even damaging effects on the children who are supposed to be served.

Many professionals in different agencies all work for children but this work is rarely coordinated and there are often tensions which arise from the different intellectual traditions that characterize these agencies. Such tensions do little to help the inclusion of children at school or in the wider society. Indeed, lack of effective cooperation can increase the push to exclusion, as agencies seek to move children and their problems to another agency.

The point that Caroline Roaf makes in this book is that when failure occurs at school, or when children clash with authority, the antecedents are usually multifarious yet connected: poverty, abuse, inconsistent care and illness often figure in the biographies of children who fail at school or get into trouble. Yet the complexity of the origins of children's difficulties is rarely recognized in the response of the 'boxed up' helping systems. The response of the school is often one-dimensional, following the furrows of the special systems which have been developed by disciplinary tradition and professional practice. It is the separateness of the latter which militates against inclusion. The response, reflecting the organization of these special services, is often to try to disaggregate children's difficulties – educational, medical, social, criminal – when in fact these difficulties are interconnected and inseparable. Separate, special systems create separate, special children catered for by special classes, special schools, special care systems and custody.

All of these mean exclusion from the mainstream. Only by recognizing the integrated nature of children's difficulties will inclusion be possible and this recognition can arise only from improved inter-agency understanding – from the 'joined up thinking' and 'joined up services' of recent government rhetoric. In this book Caroline Roaf moves beyond the rhetoric to clear advice on how to make coordination happen.

Gary Thomas
Christine O'Hanlon

Preface

I first became aware of the need for inter-agency work as a magistrate in Oxford City in the late 1970s. Every day a number of adult homeless petty offenders and street drinkers would appear in court and a great deal of energy was spent working out alternatives to imprisonment for people with 'no fixed abode', no money to pay a fine and no prospect of employment. As lay people, magistrates did not have the answers, but nor, it seemed, did the probation officers, social workers and solicitors attending court to speak on behalf of their 'difficult to place' clients. No one seemed able to offer the court any positive solutions for the care of petty offenders for whom prison was clearly not the answer. The frustration felt by agencies, particularly probation officers and magistrates, over their combined failure to solve this problem led to the formation of an inter-agency working party under the auspices of a local charity for ex-offenders, the Elmore Committee. This group, chaired by a fellow magistrate, Patricia Vereker (to whose memory this book is dedicated), consisted of representatives from the probation service, social services, the health service and the magistracy. It met regularly to work on the problem of the lack of provision for difficult to place people, each of whom challenged the ability of agencies to work together. As a member of that group, and as a special educational needs teacher, the parallels between the problems agencies faced in relation to 'difficult to place' adults and those teachers faced in relation to 'through the net' children were obvious. Therapeutic interventions for young offenders, such as Intermediate Treatment, familiar in the 1970s, had lost favour as sentencing options by the early nineties and truancy and disaffection were increasing. It seemed a small step to replicate the project for 'difficult to place' people, in a new project to improve inter-agency cooperation for children and young people. This book is about the insights gained from that experience.

Since 1985, when I became a member of the Elmore Committee's working party, I have had the opportunity to meet and work with many people from a wide range of agencies, statutory and non-statutory. Many still work locally and I owe them all my most sincere thanks for their help, advice and support over the years and for their continued efforts to work together on behalf of children and young people in Oxfordshire. It would be impossible to name them all here: those mentioned must stand as their representatives.

My first thanks go to Patricia Vereker, Pat Goodwin, Christopher Bradley and Blue Tewson, who were my mentors and whose thinking and professional practice have been a constant source of inspiration and encouragement. I am grateful to the headteachers and schools I have worked in over the period for their support of inter-agency work, and to Liz Brighouse, Director of Oxfordshire Council for Voluntary Action, for her willingness to 'house' the inter-agency project, described here as Elmore II, during the period when it was supported financially by the Joseph Rowntree Foundation. For this support and the advice and help provided by Barbara Ballard, Senior Research Officer at the Joseph Rowntree Foundation, and the members of the advisory group appointed by the Foundation I am deeply grateful. Especial and affectionate thanks are due to the members of the project's steering group for their commitment through thick and thin over the five years the project was in operation, and above all to Cathy Lloyd, the project's courageous and dedicated research and development officer whose own contribution to the literature on inter-agency cooperation I am delighted to acknowledge here.

Especial thanks are due to Georgina Glenny, whose own involvement with Elmore II and III is longstanding and whose advice and encouragement over the years have steered me through what seemed, at times, an impossibly daunting task. I am grateful, too, to Gary Thomas and colleagues at Oxford Brookes University, for much advice and encouragement in taking the ideas discussed here further. Finally, I thank my family for putting up with neglect and Dermot for endless nourishment.

Caroline Roaf

List of abbreviations

ACPC	area child protection committee
AWPU	age weighted pupil unit
CRDU	Children's Rights Development Unit
CYP	Children and Young People
DES	Department of Education and Science
DfE	Department for Education
DfEE	Department for Education and Employment
DfES	Department for Education and Skills
DHSS	Department of Health and Social Security
DTP	difficult to place
EAZ	Education Action Zone
ECST	Elmore Community Support Team
ESW	education social worker
HMSO	Her Majesty's Stationery Office
IT	intermediate treatment
JCC	joint consultative committee
JRF	Joseph Rowntree Foundation
LEA	local education authority
LMS	local management of schools
MARS	Mobile Action Resource Service
MPA	multiprofessional assessment
NARE	National Association for Remedial Education
NCB	National Children's Bureau
NFER	National Foundation for Educational Research
OECD	Organisation for Economic Co-operation and Development
Ofsted	Office for Standards in Education
ROSLA	raising of the school leaving age
TTN	through the net

SEN	special educational needs
SENCO	special educational needs coordinator
SENSS	special educational needs support service
SIS	Social Information Services
SLG	school liaison group
TIC	Training for Interprofessional Collaboration
YST	Youth Support Team

CHAPTER ONE

'Through the net' children and young people: challenge and opportunity

This book is about the contribution inter-agency work for children and young people makes to the process and progress of inclusion, where 'agencies' are the state and voluntary systems that provide legally mandated or other services or voluntary help. For many years it has been recognized that cooperation is needed in relation to young people in difficulty but until recently there has been more evidence of the failure of agencies to cooperate than of their success in this (Audit Commission 1994, 1996; Parsons *et al.* 1994; Kendrick *et al.* 1996). Indeed, problems of communication and coordination continue to hamper the development of human service agencies, resulting in misery and waste of resources. The issues addressed over the years are the familiar ones of homelessness, child protection, adolescent mental health, young offenders, special educational needs and children 'looked after' and leaving care. There are lessons to be learnt from the past which suggest ways forward in what continues to be, for many practitioners, a challenging endeavour, albeit one now endorsed by government.

Although schools and education services (for example, psychologists and education social workers), social services, health professionals, the police and charities all work for children, this work remains notoriously difficult to coordinate and there are often tensions which arise from the different professional and intellectual traditions that characterize these agencies.

When professionals engage in boundary disputes over responsibility for a child, much time and effort is dissipated in bureaucratic activities rather than in making a combined effort to ensure the young person's attendance and progress at school and well-being at home. Boundary disputes do nothing to help the inclusion of children at school or in the wider society.

When children fare poorly at school, this is rarely the consequence of a single underlying condition. Failure may be the result of either a sequence, or combination, of adverse circumstances. Young people, identified in many studies, who tend not to receive appropriate support in such circumstances are variously:

- carers;
- on the verge of criminality;
- having mental health problems;
- homeless;
- out of school for any length of time;
- experiencing education difficulties while being looked after by the local authority;
- from families in stress;
- experiencing delays in assessment or provision through the process leading to a statement under the 1981 Education Act (Roaf and Lloyd 1995).

Estimating the size of the population of such young people at risk is difficult, since there is no generally accepted definition. For example, a study of 17 OECD member countries, of which the UK was one, found an estimate of between 15 and 30 per cent being reported as 'at risk', identifying groups similar to those above (OECD 1995). Behind each of the individuals in the groups listed lies a history of personal need for care extending into, and emanating from, their families and the communities in which they live. The lessons learnt from attending to their needs could contribute greatly to agencies' understanding of how to work more effectively with everyone.

Despite the complexity of their difficulties, in school, teachers often find that when professionals work closely together, young people reach their educational potential. Experience of this collaborative endeavour, learnt in difficult circumstances, can be drawn on to help agencies work together to provide better services for all children. It is argued here, on the basis of such evidence, that inclusion depends more than is fully appreciated on the ability of agencies not only to cooperate, but to go further and coordinate their services.

This book aims to identify, over time and in agency and professional practice, what contributes to, or inhibits, the development of effective models of inter-agency practice. The evaluation of existing practice is an exercise still regarded by some as problematic (Lewis and Utting 2001). An understanding of the factors underlying successful models of inter-agency practice is part of what is required to ensure that the evaluation of existing inter-agency practice becomes more effective. Given that the failure to cooperate challenges a democratic society and basic human rights, and in view of the time and attention already devoted to this subject over a number of years, this expectation is not unreasonable.

A starting point is to examine some of the beliefs held by agency members on the subject of inter-agency work in relation to children and young people. In my own case, as a practitioner, the beliefs I held about inter-agency work in this area were derived from experience. Among these were ideas such as:

- Inter-agency cooperation is essential in order to provide the support and provision required by those whose needs cannot be met by one service alone.

- Inter-agency cooperation is an important means of maintaining community safety.
- Inter-agency cooperation has an important part to play in achieving social justice. Conversely, the failure to cooperate leads to injustice in terms of misdirection of resources and loss of opportunity.
- 'Problems' lie in the failure of agencies to cooperate, rather than in the young people themselves.
- The models, methodology and process appropriate for one group can in principle be transferred to other groups.

In practice, however, these beliefs conflicted with others, such as that:

- Inter-agency cooperation, however desirable, is very difficult to achieve.
- The current level of inter-agency cooperation is satisfactory as it is.
- Inter-agency cooperation is a dangerous concept since it encourages agencies to relinquish responsibility for clients they perceive as challenging.

In addition to the conflicting beliefs held by agency members about inter-agency work, there was confusion (discussed in more detail later) about what words such as cooperation, collaboration and coordination mean. Joined up thinking implies a degree of cooperation. However, those on the receiving end of services are more likely to be interested in whether or not such cooperation results in 'joined up' (i.e. coordinated) action.

Case histories of individual young people added to the confusion. For example, some young people, whose personal circumstances might lead one to expect a coordinated response from a range of agencies, seemed to have managed to overcome their difficulties and enter 'normal' adult life without it. In short, some young people were not seriously disadvantaged by the failure of agencies to work together, while for others this led to loss of life chances and, became, in some situations, life threatening.

This book focuses on strategies to improve the life chances of those who fall 'through the net' of agency provision. There are two reasons for this. First, study of the most challenging situations frequently suggests strategies of universal value and application. Sustainable inter-agency coordination is essential to safeguard both the lives and the life chances of some of the most vulnerable young people in society. There are very few cases of, for example, death from child abuse or child on child murder in which the failure of agencies to cooperate is not cited as a contributory factor. While playing an important part in the bigger picture – that is, the success of the current movement towards a more inclusive society – inter-agency work can be, literally, a vital force in the day-to-day lives of excluded, life-chance-threatened young people.

Second, education is in a somewhat anomalous situation in relation to the other two primary care services. Where health and social services would be expected to prioritize those in most need, whose circumstances are life threatening, the education services, a lack of which threaten life chances, if not life itself, have no such demand made upon them. Inter-agency cooperation has a key role to play in addressing this glaring inconsistency. 'Triage', as practised in medicine, to sort and prioritize those in greatest need, should have no place in the education services. Triage, as a procedure,

> is most extreme in emergency and crisis situations where the overriding goal is to identify those who require urgent treatment but are not so severely injured that survival is unlikely whatever aid they receive . . . Some people may have such severe injuries that, given the constraints of the situation (where there are insufficient resources to meet all needs) they are unlikely to survive even with additional attention: they may receive painkillers but they are not rushed into the operating theatre. In effect they are allowed to die. These decisions would be unthinkable under normal circumstances, but are made in response to a prioritisation of need in relation to current circumstances and finite resources.
>
> (Gillborn 2001: 108)

Unfortunately, the application of the principle of triage in education means that some young people move from positions in which life chances are threatened to positions in which the risk is to life itself.

'Through the net' is a phrase often used metaphorically of clients by agency workers in circumstances where they recognize the need for cooperation between agencies to provide a network of support, but have been frustrated in their attempts to achieve this. Agency workers also express concern about an unknown number of young people who are never referred to any agency for action but are none the less caught sight of fleetingly at some point in their careers, perhaps as persistent truants from school in their mid-teens, or homeless. Later, when recounting their past histories, it becomes clear that had they been referred, or referred themselves, for professional assistance, they would have been considered eligible. It appears, therefore, that clients fall 'through the net' when individual primary care agencies:

1 Try to do on their own what can only be achieved by cooperation.
2 Fail to do anything because, in their view, the client's needs should be met by some other agency.
3 Only do what they can do on their own.

In the first case too many practitioners are involved, independently of each other. The help offered may be contradictory or involve duplication. The client may not be 'through the net' to begin with, but usually ends up becoming so. This might be because the young person has outgrown agency responsibility – for example, by leaving school – or agencies may give up through exhaustion, lack of resources or reprioritization of case loads. For example, a local education social work service may decide, as a matter of policy, to reduce pressure on truants turning 16 in order to increase it on younger pupils. The net effect of having too many people involved independently of each other causes waste of resources, frustration, 'case meeting rage' and lack of trust between agencies.

In the second and third cases, too few people are involved and the client loses. In the short term agencies may gain because no resources are used. In the long term, however, they lose through lack of public confidence in their services. Society also loses, through the burden of increased tax and insurance. The failure of agencies to deal with potentially difficult situations at an early stage can result in very expensive intervention and/or risk to life or property later on. For example, the cost to agencies of a 16-year-old in court for three substantive charges of theft and 100 offences taken into consideration might not exceed £1,000, but the cost to society may be in excess of £100,000. At present there are very few strategies to prevent the long-term cost to society caused by short-term failure to respond to initial expressions of concern.

'Through the netness', and the frustration associated with it, is not a state ascribed to their clients only by agency workers involved with young people. Other constellations of agencies working with other groups experience the same phenomenon and similarly ascribe 'through the netness' to a minority of their clients. The focus here is on the agencies involved with young people, but there are lessons to be learned from similar studies focusing on other agencies in relation to other groups which will be of mutual significance to them all. The inter-agency project described in Chapter 4 leant heavily, for example, on the work of a local group set up in the mid-1980s to meet the needs of adult mentally disordered homeless offenders. Personal experience of this early project suggested that effective inter-agency practice relied on certain roles, tasks and skills carried out within a framework designed to promote effective communication. More knowledge about the detail of this framework might therefore hold the key to the promotion of good practice more widely.

If children and young people at risk of falling 'through the net' constitute a major challenge to the primary care agencies, they are no less challenging to the researcher. Virtually every writer on inter-agency cooperation and every government or independent report (Seebohm 1968; Jaques 1986; Butler-Sloss 1988; Gill and Pickles 1989; Audit Commission 1994) on the subject speaks of both its desirability and its difficulty.

What are these difficulties and how can they be overcome? We can start by accepting that inter-agency cooperation, far from being a new idea, thought up in the 1990s, has a long history and an extensive literature going back more than thirty years. This literature covers a wide range of private and public enterprise and cooperative endeavour expressing society's concern in relation to the welfare of children and young people at risk (Mapstone 1983; Hallett and Birchall 1992). Increasingly, insights from one field of interest cross-fertilize with others, documented in a range of studies. For example, in the world of business management, writers such as Handy (1985), Hambleton *et al.* (1995), Owen (1996) and Huxham (1996) have much to contribute. In much of the literature, the practice of inter-agency cooperation is either specifically promoted, or inferred, as a means of overcoming agency difficulties in relation to vulnerable groups. Because of this long history, many professionals, still in post, began their careers with as much enthusiasm for inter-agency work as government has today. Their experience can still be called upon.

On the basis of this history, I argue that the practice of inter-agency work is at a transition stage. Having been associated for some years with isolated, usually small-scale, short-term local projects, inter-agency practice is now developing rapidly, in response to the setting up of large-scale government supported initiatives. It is now possible to generalize and to consider the development of inter-agency work as a new area of specialist expertise with its own history and body of knowledge. Interprofessionality and inter-disciplinarity reached this point some time ago (Jaques 1986; Becher 1989; Bines and Watson 1992). Inter-agency work has not, but since it subsumes interdisciplinarity and interprofessionality, lack of attention to it is holding up the progress of all three.

An offshoot of the lack of understanding of inter-agency work at practitioner level concerns the confusion between inter- and intra-agency/meetings and/ or professionalism. Education, for example, employs a large number of professionals from different disciplines, such as psychology or social work. When they meet together, no matter how diverse the gathering, they still do so as members of an *intra*-agency group. If the meeting takes place under the auspices of education, and is composed primarily of professionals from education with only one member from social services or health, this would still, in terms of power relations, be an *intra*- rather than an *inter*-agency meeting. At an inter-agency meeting, by contrast, on whatever territory it takes place (though a neutral venue is preferred, or one which rotates round the agencies), the expectation is that all the relevant agencies will be represented and have an equal voice. It is important to be clear about this distinction, since many of the problems of inter-agency work arise because of issues to do with territory and perceived inequality in power relations. The health service and the education service are notable for having a highly differentiated workforce which includes many different professionals as well as different kinds of institution and/or units. Many of the problems associated with inter-agency work are replicated within single agencies and, where these are a feature, within their institutions. 'Through the netness' can thus occur within an agency and its institutions as easily as it occurs between them.

Part 1 of this book considers the antecedents in the case for inter-agency work as a strategy to improve services for children and young people. The current emphasis on joined up thinking is set in its historical, legislative and political context, demonstrating the length of time the issues have been identified and the extensive discussion, research and decision-making that has already taken place. Thus the development of inter-agency work spans the period from Beveridge's 'seamless web' of provision to the present day plethora of inter-agency projects and training opportunities. Nonetheless, the need for effective, sustainable models of inter-agency cooperation in relation to children and young people remains. Furthermore, this need continues to be expressed, in recent literature, and among practitioners currently working in the field, despite all that has gone on before.

Part 1 also considers the implications of inter-agency work for agencies, professionals and young people, to establish what it is about agencies as organizations, and professionals and their co-workers as individuals, that promotes or inhibits the collaboration so many of them profess to want and their clients appear to need. What, we might ask, is standing in the way of it, in terms of legislation and agency response?

Part 2 explores inter-agency work in practice and analyses this in the light of the factors drawn from the history of legislation promoting inter-agency work, and the development of agency and professional practice outlined in Chapters 2 and 3. Chapter 4 records some research carried out over the ten-year transition period between the small-scale projects of the early 1990s and the large-scale inter-agency projects of the new millennium. An inter-agency project, set up to investigate the problems faced by agencies in their work with children and young people at risk of falling 'through the net', is outlined. In Chapter 5 this project is compared with other similar contemporaneous projects to identify characteristics of good practice. The implications of these examples are discussed in Chapter 6. They suggest that successful inter-agency projects set up to meet the needs of those at risk of falling through the net follow a characteristic pattern. In successful and sustainable projects, collaborative activity takes place at three interconnected levels:

- policy and planning;
- implementation, case work, research and training;
- networking/liaison.

Projects supported at all three levels, it is suggested, are more likely to be successful and survive than those which are not. This pattern can be replicated in different contexts, within and between agencies and institutions, and with different client groups, to ensure effective coordination and some redistribution of resources, and to hold a balance between preventative work in relation to all children, and proactive case work on behalf of individuals at risk. These key elements structure communication pathways within and between agencies to ensure that work in relation to particular issues and individuals is coordinated, the interpersonal skills of participants are developed and policy-makers receive feedback.

In Chapters 7 and 8, inter-agency case management and the development of intra-agency teams are examined as a means of exploring these ideas further. It is suggested here that there are important, but unrecognized, similarities between the model proposed for effective inter-agency coordination and that already being developed by special educational needs teams operating in local education authorities and in mainstream schools.

The concluding chapter considers the practical implications for the future. The pattern of inter-agency working, grounded in the community, that emerges from this study is presented as the beginning of a process which would enable agencies to integrate universal and targeted provision more effectively. Although the implications for education are particularly important in view of the number of children and young people who continue to be excluded from school or who fail to attend, it is possible that models successful for children have wider application. Individual children and young people, although perceived by practitioners as being at risk of falling 'through the net', can also be construed as symptoms of a problem or set of problems similarly at risk of falling 'through the net' of agency attention, commitment and skilled intervention.

According to Clarke and Stewart (1997: 1), 'wicked issues', a concept long familiar in the States, include:

- environmental issues and an aspiration to sustainable development;
- problems of crime and an aspiration to safe communities;
- problems of discrimination and an aspiration to an equitable society;
- problems of poverty and an aspiration to a more meaningful life.

Hodgkin and Newell (1996: 32) apply the term to policy problems dealing with 'intractably complex issues where the nature of the problem and the solution are not fully understood, and which involve more than one department and are not dealt with satisfactorily by any.' If that is the case then it is not unreasonable to suppose that there is some potential for inter-agency work as part of the solution to the 'wicked issues' threatening the development of inclusive societies. It follows, as this study suggests, that inter-agency work should become, and there are signs that this is already the case, a new area of professional and para-professional expertise for which there is, as yet, little research or training. I hope this book will encourage the development of both.

PART ONE

Inter-agency perspectives

CHAPTER TWO

Developing policy

Over the past thirty years, discourse and policy formulation on this issue have changed in scale and form. There has been a move from the Olympian overview and patrician manner of the great chairs of government commit- tees of the 1960s and 1970s, such as Kilbrandon, Plowden and Seebohm, to the more recent pragmatism of the Audit Commission and the big charitable trusts such as the National Children's Bureau or the Joseph Rowntree Foun- dation. The documentary evidence reveals a cycle moving from the universal provision of the 1960s, the positive action of the 1970s and 1980s, to a reworked, 'market economy' version of universal provision once more emer- ging in the late 1990s. Appearing through this reworking is a developing concept of children as citizens, deserving a decent environment, rather than as 'objects' to receive benefits if 'need' can be identified.

Political commentators, educational theorists and philosophers such as Hutton (1995), Gewirtz *et al.* (1995) and Warnock (1998) note the shift, over the same period, from welfare state to market economy, and from needs to rights as dominating political themes. Accompaning these changes has been a widening gap between rich and poor. Among the worst affected have been children, one-third of whom, by the mid-nineties, lived in poverty (Kumar 1993, Bradshaw 2001). In addition, environmental and public health issues have increased the risks all children are exposed to (Holtermann 1996). Furthermore, the proposal that 'child impact statements' become obligatory on all policy makers as a matter of course (Freeman 1987) has not yet been achieved (Hancox 1999). Any legislative attempts to create a better life for children in difficulty must be judged against these basic facts.

This chapter traces the development of inter-agency cooperation over time and covers a number of agencies, notably education, health, social work, criminal justice, housing and probation. Four post-Second World War phases encapsulate developments in legislation and enquiry which have a direct bearing on inter-agency work in relation to young people.

From social welfare to social cohesion: post-Second World War to 1970

The post-Second World War project to tackle class division, inequality and deprivation began with the Beveridge Report in 1942, 'based on the principle of universalism in which each person was to receive according to their need rather than their ability to pay' (Welton 1989). Two Acts mark the end of the period and are landmarks in respect of developing welfare systems and positive attitudes towards children:

- The 1970 Local Authority Social Services Act unified the work previously undertaken by a range of personal social service departments.
- The 1970 Education (Handicapped Children) Act, ensured that, for the first time, *all* children, however serious their disability, were included in the education framework, where previously, under the 1944 Education Act, some had been deemed ineducable.

During the 1960s, reports, White Papers and Acts concerning the welfare, education and health of children and families leapfrog over each other, wrestling with these issues, in an attempt to examine root causes and to legislate for better practice. The rapid increase in juvenile offending acted as both an indictment and a warning – proof of the failure of what had gone before and the difficulties to be faced to improve matters in the future. Twenty-five years after Beveridge, the architects of the welfare state's 'seamless web' of provision must have hoped for something better. Nonetheless, these key themes account for a range of reports and government measures in which the need for multi-agency working and holistic approaches to family services, and the role of education are constantly reiterated. Of these, the reports of the Kilbrandon (1964), Plowden (1967) and Seebohm (1968) Committees are considered here, as is the rise of the comprehensive school.

The Kilbrandon Committee, set up 'to consider the provision of the law of Scotland relating to the treatment of juvenile delinquents and juveniles in need of care or protection or beyond parental control' (Kilbrandon 1964: para. 1), held that 'Delinquency is predominantly an activity of the young' and proposed early intervention and 'the application of an educative principle' which 'seeks to establish the individual child's needs in the light of the fullest possible information as to his circumstances, both personal and environmental' (para. 78).

Kilbrandon's proposals led to the establishment of the Scottish Children's Hearing system, a system unique to Scotland in which a lay panel reached decisions on treatment. Its key principles were that the needs of the child were the first and primary consideration, that the family played a vital role in tackling children's problems and that a preventive and educational approach should be adopted in coping with these problems.

For Kilbrandon, juvenile delinquency indicated a failure of upbringing and therefore of social education. The Report recommended the establishment of a social education department, to coordinate 'information about all cases of children in need' (para. 235). Although this was not implemented, the idea of an enlarged education authority catering for 'the needs of all children requiring measures of special education and training' (para. 241: 2), which would integrate a number of separate services, continues to generate discussion. Similar thinking is reflected, for example, in Hertfordshire's move to create a new service for children, schools and families from the previously separated education and social services (Hertfordshire County Council 2001).

Following Kilbrandon, the 1968 Seebohm Report reviewed local authority personal social services to consider the changes needed to ensure an effective family service. Seebohm, echoing Kilbrandon, sought to 'support the family, forestall and reduce delinquency and revise law and practice relating to young offenders in England and Wales' (p. 30).

The Plowden Report (1967) acknowledged its debt to Kilbrandon and relied on Seebohm to make recommendations compatible with its own in relation to health services, child care, probation and social services. It welcomed the introduction of an element of social work training in the training of health visitors and doctors. In Plowden's view, a comprehensive social work service closely related to schools would support children in their homes as part of an effective family service and would appeal to schools because of their 'need to identify and help families with difficulties that lead to poor performance and behaviour' (para. 243). Social workers would be:

> readily available to teachers, capable of assuming responsibilities for cases beyond the competence, time or training of the head or class teacher, and capable of securing help quickly from more specialised social services . . . teams should be established to include experienced workers from the relevant fields including social workers largely responsible for school social work.
>
> (para. 255)

Following Seebohm's proposals, local authority social service departments, under social services committees, were set up by the 1970 Local Authority Social Services Act to provide a unified service bringing together work previously done by a range of services: children's departments, welfare departments, education welfare, home help services, mental health social services, adult training centres, day nurseries and many others. These proposals arose primarily from concerns about the family and the waste of resources that resulted from fragmentation and overlapping: 'there could be three or four people coming into the home' (Seebohm 1989: 4). For Seebohm, since the family was 'everybody, whether of one or a large family' (p. 3), the service had to be a comprehensive family-based service, not just a service dealing with children and old people:

> in a school, for instance, where the teacher sees a child who is apparently withdrawn, who is occasionally absent, who is badly clothed, who looks ill; here are symptoms. This could be referred to someone dealing only with children. But when you look into this . . . you may find the most appalling housing conditions . . . the parents estranged . . . or alcoholic . . . another child who is abnormal, and so on, causing stress to

the family. This means a great number of departments will have to be involved . . . the housing department, the health department, the education department, the children's department . . . With that divided responsibility nobody is clearly responsible for this family problem.

(Seebohm 1989: 4)

In the field of criminal justice, the 1969 Children and Young Person's Act originated, like Kilbrandon, in the debates of the late 1950s and 1960s concerning the care of juveniles through the courts and the accommodation needs of children in care and fostered. These concerns found expression in legislation and reports promoting the welfare of children by helping them and their families in the community. Further reports and White Papers through the 1960s (Home Office 1962, 1965) confirmed a rising political interest in juvenile crime.

Jones and Kerslake (1979: 3) consider that the emphasis in these documents:

was on providing a family social work service as an antidote to delinquency. The recommendation was that family councils should replace juvenile courts. This was intended to reduce the stigma attached to court attendance and to allow more flexibility in meeting the changing needs of children and young people. These proposals were implemented in Scotland as part of the Social Work (Scotland) Act, 1968, where there was not the same inter-departmental squabbles, and inter-party conflicts, over these radical proposals as there was in England and Wales.

They point out that in England and Wales, responsibility for child care services and for penal policy lay with the Home Office, whereas other social work services were the responsibility of the recently created department of Health and Social Security.

In respect of children and young people up to the age of 17, the 1969 Children and Young Person's Act introduced the concept of intermediate treatment (IT) as a sentencing option, and as a statutory responsibility for social services. The courts were empowered, when making a supervision order, to include the requirement that the child participate in 'specified activities' limited to a maximum of 90 days in any one year, of a type approved by the Secretary of State for Social Services and supervised by either a social worker or a probation officer.

IT was intended to enable children to be treated in their own communities with others of their own age, not necessarily delinquent. It was regarded as consistent with earlier proposals for a social work service which would secure an effective family service. There were, however, other factors at work. According to Hall (1976: 33):

For those interested in achieving more fundamental changes than those just concerning delinquency, the issue of juvenile crime is useful as a springboard. By arguing that the prevention of juvenile delinquency is preferable to cure and that the former can only be achieved by a widespread improvement in social services, it is possible to construct a case for more general reforms. In the policy developments in both England

and Wales, and Scotland, those interested in promoting a family service used the issue of juvenile delinquency to further their cause.

Jones and Kerslake (1979: 2) also saw a growing awareness of deprivation and disadvantage:

The post war euphoria of the 1950s . . . was eclipsed by an awareness of poverty and inequality at a time when many had 'never had it so good'. There was an ideological bud-burst, this was the time of flower power and hippies, of love, peace and freedom. Man was seen as being restricted by his social and cultural environment . . . there was also a growing political interest by many young people. Campaigns against the Vietnam War, the riots of 1968 in Paris, the proliferation of pressure groups.

IT, they considered, was a relevant response for three main reasons. First, delinquency was a major political and media concern in the 1960s. Second, the changing social values of the 1960s, expressed in the 1969 Act, were based on a perception of children as deprived rather than depraved. Third, the social context of the 1960s promoted the idea of care rather than control, and treatment rather than punishment.

At the time, IT as a sentencing option encouraged many areas to produce local schemes and projects for young people and encouraged some community groups to include more challenging youngsters in their programmes. However, gradually through the 1970s IT began to be seen by powerful elements among the judiciary as a soft option. Instead, increasing numbers of juveniles were detained, social workers were regarded as unrealistically soft on crime and magistrates were increasingly concerned by the number of children out of control while in local authority care. The debate generated by IT at the time and subsequently, as to who should receive it and what part it might play in community-based social work service for adolescents, is an issue no less live today than it was twenty years ago. Was it to be for a small minority of deprived children, or for those who had been before the courts, or for everyone? For Jones and Kerslake (1979: 9), it was 'an umbrella term for a wide range of both actual and potential community-based provision for adolescents (and children) who are deprived or who are more "at risk" of getting into trouble than their contemporaries.' For them, IT offered the adolescent: 'a package that is more intensive in terms of time, impact, and effect. Day care, alternative schooling, and short term, focused, residential care might all be included in an intensive intermediate treatment programme' (Jones and Kerslake 1979: 11). Despite the demise of IT as a component in court orders, the continued development of the concept and its tenaciousness as a therapeutic strategy for agencies working with vulnerable and challenging young people has been notable, re-emerging in our own day in initiatives such as Connexions (DfES 2001a).

Finally, the development of the comprehensive school (DES 1965) brought together a number of different professionals from a range of social backgrounds, who then had to confront difficulties of communication and cooperation, and differences in professional culture. A mid-1970s study of four comprehensive schools (Johnson *et al.* 1980: 182) looked at how they cared for their pupils and how the balance was to be maintained 'between being part of a wider welfare network and providing the specialised professional service of secondary education'.

By 1970, the post-Beveridge generation had seen young people and their families move from post-war austerity to increasing prosperity and an explosion of individualism – the 'doing your own thing' of the 1960s. Education, health and the personal social services were developing in new ways both structurally and professionally, stimulated by the idealistic holism of government reports such as Kilbrandon, Plowden and Seebohm. Meanwhile, questions of accountability, responsibility and the use of public funds escaped public scrutiny less easily, with an increasing interest in the management and coordination of public services. In this respect the Kilbrandon proposals and philosophy played a key role in their emphasis on preventative work in the development of the Scottish juvenile justice system. According to Gill and Pickles (1989): 'It may be that the Scottish system of large regional authorities, child centred practices and the consensus framework of the children's hearings, have all contributed uniquely to a climate which is conducive to such [inter-agency] initiatives (Introduction).'

Humanitarian concern for those in need or at risk was beginning, however, to be tempered by realism. Naive beliefs that problems would go away with sufficient welfare or that there were not difficult choices to be made about the spending of public money could not be sustained. Considerations of this kind were partly responsible for Plowden's view that new money would have to be found to support Educational Priority Areas, and Seebohm's concern not to waste resources. Why should three or more professionals descend on one family in need when one key worker would do? To ease the tension between the need for one key worker and increasing specialization, professionals could see that cooperation was needed and could be achieved through teamwork.

1970–1988: equal opportunities

During the 1970s concerns of a different kind emerged. The 1975 Race Relations Act and the 1976 Sex Discrimination Act, followed by the 1981 Education Act and the Swann Report (1985), assert the rights of minority groups, including children, to self-determination and to justice and equality in law. The period saw the transition from selection and segregation to integration and inclusion, from a concept of equality which treated everyone as if they were the same to a concept which valued diversity and social justice. Society as a whole had to grapple with the contradictions in these radically different positions. The rhetoric of equal opportunities wore thin as individuals and pressure groups began to confront the lack of social justice which made a mockery of 'opportunity'. However, positive action implies the development of reliable measures and definitions of need so that resources can be targeted effectively. Some of the most heated debates of the 1980s were about the ethics of ethnic monitoring and the categorization of children with special educational needs (Barton and Tomlinson 1981; Stone 1981; Taylor 1981; Tomlinson 1982). In this context it became apparent that positive action was not in itself sufficient. The Fish Report (1985: 2.14.60), echoing Warnock (1978), concluded that:

> services for all children should be provided within the same comprehensive framework and should only be special in the sense that it properly meets the needs of the child not special in that it is a different service or a service provided in a different place.

These dilemmas are clearly demonstrated in education. The bringing together of previously segregated children under one roof revealed the continuum of need and the close relationship and impact of non-educational problems on educational needs. This made nonsense of education legislation to separate these. Nor was the desire to promote inter-agency and inter-professional cooperation helped by the 1974 local government and health services reorganization. The Warnock Report (1978: para. 15.2) was probably typical in remarking that 're-organisation made co-operation [between services], at a local level, which we seek to promote, more rather than less difficult'. Reasoning of this sort may account for the shortage of inter-agency initiatives at the time and the interest expressed in joint consultative committees (JCCs) by both Warnock and the 1976 Court Report on Child Health Services.

JCCs were set up by the 1973 National Health Service Act to promote a joint community approach to consider and advise the three primary care services on the planning, provision and coordination of arrangements in their areas. For Court (1976) and Warnock (1978), JCCs had the potential to play a key role in relation to children and families. Court recommended 'a child and family centred service, in which skilled help is readily available and accessible; which is integrated in as much as it sees the child as a whole, and as 'a continuously developing person' (p. 368). Court emphasized, as did Warnock, that 'Many of the children with the most complex problems, and the most severe handicaps will require help from all three services [education, health and social services] . . . The planning and development of an integrated health service must therefore be done in such a way as to facilitate at every level the closest possible working relationships with these other services' (Warnock 1978: para. 5.25). Children, the Court Report declared, in a ringing defence of children's rights, 'are full citizens with an equal right to health and to health services whatever their age and wherever they live' (para. 5.19).

Warnock regarded JCCs 'as vital for the *co-ordination* and development of services for children and young people with disabilities or significant difficulties' (para. 15.49, emphasis added). This is spelt out more fully in para. 16.49:

> the machinery which we have proposed for the co-ordination of services at different levels should provide a framework which will facilitate day

to day contact between members of different professions at working level on matters of common concern, make for greater efficiency, extend horizons and promote development.

A framework was particularly required within which to implement the Warnock Report's proposal concerning the multiprofessional assessment (MPA) of those with severe, complex or long-term disabilities.

However, as Warnock acknowledged, JCCs 'vary considerably in effectiveness and some lack the status and prestige necessary to exert a major influence' (para. 16.30). Nevertheless, 'despite these disadvantages, we consider that the existing structure of the JCCs should be utilised to promote the co-ordination of services for children and young people with special need' (para. 16.31). Warnock (para. 16.31) duly recommended that:

working groups should be set up under the auspices of the JCCs to review the provision of and operation of services for children and young people up to the age of, say, 25 with disabilities and significant difficulties, with a view to identifying deficiencies in provision and practice, developing strategies and programmes to meet those deficiencies and, as necessary, recommending policies for improving the effectiveness of the separate services and of their co-operation with each other.

In practice, it has been difficult for JCCs to take full account of young people with emotional and behavioural difficulties, or of families suffering from stress, such as extreme poverty or homelessness. To the problems already mentioned, of effectiveness and status, could be added remoteness from practitioners and clients, and lack of funding. Furthermore, as a health service initiative, they were almost bound to favour health service agenda and mind sets. Warnock's observation, that it would be at the level of 'the individual doctor, teacher, nurse, social worker or other professional' that the report's recommendations on collaboration would stand or fall, is perhaps not surprising (para. 15.52), but it left a lot to chance. Similarly, the effectiveness of joint working arrangements for children with disabilities and difficulties was thought to depend on 'all concerned being well informed and aware of each other's work and able to develop the means to deal with common problems' (para. 15.52).

Also looking to JCCs in its search for a framework, the Child Guidance movement provides evidence of inter-agency cooperation taking place in practice as an undercurrent over a long period, outside the domain of formal government policy. It none the less influenced the philosophy and practice of other policy movements taking place in Britain in the 1970s and 1980s. Its progress was similarly influenced by the political and socio-economic changes of the day. Sampson (1980: 1) describes Child Guidance as 'a certain way of approaching problem behaviour in children . . . the movement was originally conceived and developed in America to deal with juvenile delinquency but was soon extended to cover other kinds of difficult or neurotic behaviour' (p. 1). The movement recognized that psychological pressures had complex social, emotional and cognitive components: 'To unravel the tangle, a group of specialists, who would pool their expertise and come up with solutions taking all the essentials of each individual case into account, seemed the answer' (p. 1). This was the origin of the basic Child Guidance team of medical psychologist (psychiatrist), educational psychologist and psychiatric social worker, who each, significantly, as we shall see later,

> separately investigates the presenting problem according to his own particular approach but diagnosis is not complete until the viewpoints have all been assimilated and discussed in conference. Later each specialist plays his appropriate part in the treatment according to the decisions mutually arrived at.
>
> (Samson 1980: 1)

Throughout the 1970s, as part of local government reorganization, 'government circulars developed the view of Child Guidance . . . as a network of services provided to help maladjusted children, each having its own base and its own professional staff, and coming together in a variety of ways when problems of maladjustment or mental ill health demanded joint action' (Wright, in Sampson 1980: 78).

Given the problems, first, over definition in relation to children with special educational needs, and, second, the coordination of services, it became clear that the coordinating structure, recommended by Warnock and regarded as 'vital', was flawed. Children and young people with disabilities could expect some benefit, but those with other significant difficulties risked falling 'through the net'. However, although coordinating structures at policy level were problematic, among middle management professionals and practitioners, multidisciplinary and multiprofessional teams were increasingly being used as a device to bring specialist professional services together to meet the increasing complexity of client need. This trend was accompanied by an increased interest in inter-professional training and inter-agency coordination and planning.

1988–1994: working together for social inclusion

While practitioners and policy-makers attempted to sort out difficulties of definition and the coordination of services, the socio-economic and political situation exerted its own pressure on all services. Resources were under threat, local government was increasingly out of favour with central government and local authorities, as major public spenders, were under scrutiny from a Tory government increasingly reluctant to support public services. Evidence continued to accumulate concerning child poverty and young homelessness as well as the more familiar concern over young offenders (Kumar 1993). In schools, there were concerns about discipline (Elton Report 1989), exclusions (DfE 1992; Parsons *et al.* 1994) and children with emotional and behavioural difficulties (DfE 1994a; Kurtz *et al.* 1994). In this climate the term inter-agency, as distinct from inter-professional, cooperation began to emerge, promoted in particular by the Report of the Inquiry into Child Abuse in Cleveland (Butler-Sloss 1988) and the 1989 Children Act.

The 1989 Children Act and its implementation shifted attention from juvenile delinquency to wider concerns about the environment in which children and young people live. Despite the lack of congruence between its aims and contemporary British political ideology, the 1989 Children Act was favourably received following the publication of the Cleveland Report in 1988. At a practical level agencies organized extensive training for their members in the implementation of the Act. For many, these initiatives awakened memories of previous practice in IT or Child Guidance. Added impetus came from the Act's origin in the United Nations Declaration on the Rights of the Child. Supporters of the Act had the confidence, therefore, of being part of an international movement to improve children's rights and welfare (Kirst 1991).

After Cleveland agencies had to accept, as did the general public, the full extent of abuse directed at children and young people. The most significant outcome was the publication of the DoH, DES and Welsh Office guide *Working Together* (1991). This proposed a standardized structure and format for new local handbooks recommending procedures to be gone through in local authorities concerning child abuse in their areas. It led to the setting up of Child Protection Registers and Panels and outlined inter-agency processes to accord with good practice. All agencies involved with children and young people were affected by this and all were required to take part in appropriate training programmes.

Cleveland thus marks a turning point in public perception of services for children, and of children themselves as 'rights bearing'. To what extent, Newell (1988: 200) asks, have 'they [professionals] respected children as people rather than objects of concern in all the talk of inter-agency teamwork and new training initiatives?' Child abuse, according to Newell, was a children's rights issue: 'it is not fundamentally a medical or social work or judicial/penal . . . child abuse is the misuse of adult power over children, a failure to respect the child's rights to autonomy, physical integrity and privacy' (p. 200).

Successful responses from the child's point of view must therefore be based on respect for the child and for children's rights principles. Newell's concern was that:

> The Cleveland affair was only the latest – although probably the most publicised – demonstration that the 'best interests' justification for intervention in children's lives can be sadly inadequate. No doubt everyone in Cleveland believed themselves to be acting in the 'best interests' of the children. But clearly in many cases – and in many, many cases outside Cleveland too – professional 'abuse' has in fact piled on top of the actual or suspected physical, sexual or emotional abuse of the child.
>
> (1988: 200)

Thus Cleveland also stands as a caution against uncritical or over-enthusiastic claims for inter-agency cooperation as a panacea for young people's difficulties unless accompanied by attention to the sometimes competing rights of children and parents.

Following Cleveland, the 1989 Children Act brought together child care law passed since the 1948 Children's Act, incorporating a new framework for the care and protection of children and seeking to give young people a greater say in the decision-making process. It was described at the time as:

> the most comprehensive piece of legislation which parliament has ever enacted about children . . . It integrates the law relating to private individuals with the responsibilities of public authorities, in particular local authority social services departments, towards children . . . the Act strikes a new balance between family autonomy and the protection of children.
> (DoH 1989: Foreword)

Among the Act's key principles was the obligation for statutory agencies such as education, social services and health to work together to promote the welfare of children and for authorities to respond as swiftly as possible in child care matters. The Act affirms that the child's welfare is paramount, that the child's wishes and feelings must be considered in any proceedings involving him or her and that the upbringing of children rests primarily with parents, with whom local authorities must work in partnership.

As an added bonus, the Act's definition of 'children in need' was one which all agencies could share. According to Section 17, a child shall be in need if:

> he is unlikely to achieve or maintain, or have the opportunity of achieving or maintaining a reasonable standard of health or development without the provision for him of services by a local authority under this Part;

> his health or development is likely to be significantly impaired, or further impaired, without the provision for him of such a service or

> he is disabled.

The Act defines 'development' as 'physical, intellectual, emotional, social or behavioural development' and 'health' as 'physical or mental health'. After the false starts of the 1981 Act's definition of 'special educational need', this offered a genuine inter-agency alternative. Although social services are given the lead role in ensuring that children and young people in need are provided for, they are expected to act in partnership with other agencies, both in the statutory and voluntary sector and to act in partnership with parents and children (Section 27). Significantly, the Act does not specify how these partnerships are to be initiated, let alone maintained.

In the political climate of the time, the 1989 Children Act was something of an anomaly. It presupposes a strong role for local authorities, respect for the wishes and feelings of children, for welfare, for cooperation and for the concept of 'society', and hit the statute book at the height of Thatcher's New Right attack on these structures and values. The United Kingdom was required, through membership of the European Union, to draw up a Children Act to commemorate thirty years since the international declaration on the Rights of the Child. The chance that legislation of this kind would have emerged then without external pressure must be regarded as slim. In the event, it provided a means by which practitioners, frustrated by government failure to support cooperative effort in society as a whole, could reassert their belief in such approaches. 'What began as consolidating legislation, attempting to draw together the many diverse threads of child care law ... became more radical and reformist during its development, as attempts were made to use the legislation to address a range of identifiable problems within the child care system' (SIS 1993: 1).

Incidents such as the 'pindown experience' in Staffordshire in 1990 highlighted public concern about standards and practices in residential child care. The Utting Report, *Children in the Public Care* (DoH 1991) expected the Children Act, then about to be implemented, to clarify 'the responsibility of the local authority for assisting children and families in need, and protecting and caring for children at risk' (para. 2). For Utting, 'The Act reflects a convergence of values about children as individuals in their own right, citizens enjoying legal protection ... The duty of public care is to deal with those children as if they were our own' (paras 3 and 4). The health service was recommended to 'require local authorities to produce plans for their children's services and monitor their implementation' (para. 109). Children's Services Plans were expected to reflect the role and contributions of other agencies such as education departments, health authorities and the police (para. 4.18).

What could not have been easily foreseen in 1989 was how quickly attention would focus once again on the figures for truancy and permanent exclusion from school (Lovey *et al.* 1993; Parsons *et al.* 1994; University of North London Truancy Unit 1994). The 1988 and 1993 Acts created the conditions for a market in schooling and relied on the rhetoric of increased parental choice to achieve it. New types of schools were to be created and information about them made available to parents so that they could exercise 'choice'. The result was the publication, obligatory under the 1993 Education Act, of so-called 'league tables' of attendance and exclusion records, as well as examination results. However unhelpful the publication of these data proved to be, there were benefits for researchers who, for the first time, had access to data on school attendance and exclusion, much of which had previously gone unrecorded: the figures were sobering.

However, the notion of the market also 'reversed any continuing trend in government policy based on the strong theory of equal opportunity' (Little and Tomlinson 1993: 161). School budgets came to depend on the number of pupils enrolled and schools therefore had to recruit to survive. Schools tended to take the view that truants, disruptive students, students with emotional and behavioural difficulties and those unlikely to succeed in public examinations would tarnish their image in the market place. In its report on provision for children with special educational needs the Audit Commission (1992a: para. 109), for example, found that: 'some headteachers are reported to be anxious to improve the disciplinary image of their school and hence are readier to exclude difficult pupils.' The 1981 Act definition of special educational need, perpetuated in the 1993 Act, did not help since it gave schools scope to be selective about whose needs they met. As a consequence, schools learned to use a number of avoidance tactics. They could decide that a child with needs did not have 'learning' difficulties and therefore had no need of additional resources. Even if it was agreed that there were learning difficulties, the school could still decide that meeting them in an ordinary school was incompatible with 'the effective use of resources' (1981 Education Act, Section 2).

The question of permanent exclusion raises a number of issues relevant for this study, since it leads to the removal of the student from the school roll. Alternative provision then has to be made by the LEA. There are sometimes lengthy delays in completing exclusion procedures and in securing alternative provision for excluded pupils. Given that the peak age for exclusion is 15, this means that a young person may not receive any significant education during the crucially important run up to GCSE.

> The aim for all excluded pupils should be to secure their early return to mainstream education. Where for whatever reason, that is not immediately possible or practicable, the provision of effective alternative education . . . is of great importance . . . without it . . . their personal happiness, fulfilment and job prospects as adults may also be adversely affected and some of them may drift into crime.
>
> (DfE 1992: para. 18)

Guidance on 'pupils with problems', including exclusion from school (DfE 1994a), included reminders that various legal provisions required collaboration between services. Once again, there were concerns about the variation in the amount and quality of provision offered to excluded pupils (Ofsted 1993). Under the terms of the 1993 Education Act, an arrangement by which money followed a pupil permanently excluded from a mainstream school, was designed to prevent schools retaining funds for students, on-roll but not present, or off-roll and on no one else's roll. With age-weighted pupil units (AWPUs) running at approximately £1,500 per secondary aged pupil, and inner city areas in the early 1990s reporting numbers of young people not on-roll in tens and hundreds, the sums of money that never reached them must have been considerable. Suddenly inter-agency work to support these young people seemed as if it should be financially viable.

There was also concern at the number of excluded primary school children. An innovative aspect of Parsons et al.'s (1994) study of this subject is its attention to the cost of exclusion. 'Costing public services, and more particularly child care services, is a relatively recent development . . . one of the aims of addressing the cost of exclusion is to give an account of where the cost burden falls' (p. 41). Once a child has been excluded, the cost is then shunted on, to other parts of the education service, to other agencies or to the community, or all three. 'Many', the report states, 'may remain "hidden"' (p. 41), as when a mother is happy to keep an excluded child at home, thereby adding to the risk of educational failure later on or involvement in crime. The report recommends that agencies 'must liaise' to minimize cost-shunting of this kind, but they need incentives for this. It cannot be motivating to sit down with someone from another agency if you suspect costs will be shunted in your direction as a result.

The 1990s also saw increased emphasis on accountability. The reports of the Audit Commission, an important feature of this period, demonstrated, when there was little political encouragement to do so, considerable commitment to local authorities and to the welfare of young people themselves. In a series of reports (1992a, b, 1993, 1994, 1996, 1998) on the accountability of public services in relation to children in need, the Commission reiterated the importance of inter-agency cooperation. In 1990/1 approximately £1.5 billion had been spent on the 1.2 million pupils with special educational needs, including the 170,000 pupils with a formal statement of special needs (Audit Commission 1992b: 1). The Commission identified 'serious deficiencies in the identification and provision for pupils with special needs' (1992a: 5), caused by lack of clarity about what constitutes special educational needs, lack of accountability by schools and LEAs for the progress made by pupils and resources received and lack of incentives for LEAs to implement the 1981 Act.

This exposure of poor practice led directly to the development of the Code of Practice (DfE 1994b) to improve the identification and assessment of special educational needs. The Code affirmed the need for: 'close co-operation between schools, LEAs, the health services and social services departments of local authorities. The Children Act 1989 and the Education Act 1993 place duties on these bodies to help each other' (para. 2.38). In its 1994 report on the coordination of community child health and social services for children in need, the Audit Commission found that effective inter-agency working was hindered by lack of a common language and local structures to implement legislation collaboratively, and the need for education to be involved. It noted that the Act did not 'provide any specific machinery to ensure that services co-ordinate, nor (except for reviews of services for children under eight) does it set any specific requirements for them to do so' (para. 5). To fulfil the expectations of the 1989 Children Act and the NHS and Community Care Act, the Commission suggested that services must respond to, and be focused on, need:

> The Children Act requires authorities to identify 'children in need'. In areas such as education and primary preventive health care, the main task is to ensure worthwhile and well organised universal provision and encourage universal uptake. In others such as child protection, the task is to identify and provide services on a selective basis. In the latter case, failure to target means not only a waste of resources but also a failure to ensure the well-being of those children who slip through the net of universal services, or for whom universal provision is insufficient.
>
> (para. 10)

This line of thinking follows the trend we saw developing through the 1980s in which the emphasis on positive action led to more precise definition and target setting.

> The first task is to define the 'needs' that authorities should be addressing and to target them accordingly. Some services are being offered to

everyone when a selective approach would be more appropriate; but even targeted services may be provided unnecessarily. They may be imprecisely focused, or miss those who need them most because they are focused inaccurately.

(para. 43)

In general, five years after the passing of the Children Act, the Commission found that 'progress towards an inter-agency strategic approach to the full range of children's services has been disappointing except where it is mandatory' (para. 41).

Health and social services authorities had not yet determined the extent of needs in their areas and could not therefore allocate resources effectively. Service objectives were vague and outcomes unclear, particularly in community child health services, but also for children looked after by the social services. Finally, the Audit Commission could find little sign of collaboration between services, or of the inter-agency approach to strategic planning for children which had been recommended by Utting in 1991. In fact, joint children's strategies and the publication of local authority children's services plans did not become mandatory until 1997. Interestingly, the Commission did not, as it might have done, suggest that English and Welsh authorities seek advice from Scotland, where joint youth strategy was already well developed (Gill and Pickles 1989).

Primary care services for children were not alone in their need for inter-agency cooperation. A research project exploring the housing implications of community care (Arnold et al. 1993) illustrates many features in common with inter-agency initiatives working with children. Among these was the tendency for local initiatives to take place in the vacuum caused by government (local or national) inertia.

partly influenced by potential local government review, signs are emerging that some of the structural problems in linking together health, social services, housing and voluntary sector interest in community care are being overcome. In some areas the cumbersome structures of joint planning have given way to more creative, action oriented inter-agency forums seeking to develop new principles of joint working and co-ordination on a range of housing and community care issues. However for the most part, these initiatives have been taken without clear guidance from central government and very much in the style of 'do it yourself'.

(Arnold et al. 1993: 5)

According to Arnold et al., a number of factors, notably joint training, could determine the success or failure of inter-agency cooperation locally. Inter-professional and inter-agency differences and defensiveness interfered with the development of a coherent approach to community care. This included difficulties in the assessment process and frequent 'buck-passing' between agencies. There was little understanding of what each individual agency could offer and there was tension between agencies when what one agency considered appropriate could not be delivered. The development of multi-agency teams – 'seamless teams' – had provided the locus of change. 'The transitions to new ways of working which all agencies are facing offer a golden opportunity for a collaborative rethink of mutual problems and joint ownership of common principles' (Arnold *et al.* 1993: 27). However, weighed down by scarce resources, agencies were often discouraged from a consideration of the creative solutions which would help them mitigate the effect of financial crisis. Thus the existence of 'voluntary sector trouble-shooting agencies' provided 'a measure of the unwillingness of statutory authorities to take on the taxing needs of the most vulnerable people 'in the community' (p. 37).

Findings such as these from voluntary sector research and community action illustrate the strength of the commitment and 'do-it-yourself' initiative that began to emerge in the 1990s. The combination of Cleveland and the 1989 Children Act established that children's welfare had to come before the difficulties and inconveniences cooperation posed for professionals. This time whole agencies were involved and what followed became a search for effective solutions.

1994 onwards: the search for solutions

By 1994, the idea of inter-agency collaboration was well accepted, as was the idea that children and young people might 'fall through the net' of provision. However, the welfare project of the 1960s and 1970s had been superseded by the ideology of the market, and reduced expenditure on public services, with little evidence that this had advantaged more than the prosperous few. In response, pressure group activity and growing self-determination among, and on behalf of, disadvantaged groups meant that the concept of inclusion was pursued with renewed energy. Prime ministerial statements such as 'there is no such thing as society, only individuals and families' (Margaret Thatcher in 1988) set the tone. In this political climate, the problems and difficulties experienced by young people, already severe, became more so. The desire to promote inter-agency cooperation in this period can be viewed as a theoretical, problem-solving response to this situation, a device to help practitioners and policy-makers close the gap between a government seeking to secure services which will do more for less, and a voluntary sector determined to ameliorate conditions for the least well off. In some cases, agencies, with some justification, pleaded the need to protect their own essential services, rather than risk reducing these to the point of extinction by contributing to a shared inter-agency enterprise. Others, on the other hand, took advantage of the vacuum noted by Arnold *et al.* (1993) to develop more cooperative ways of working. In these circumstances, there was a strong tendency for *intra*-agency cooperation to take precedence over *inter*-agency coordination.

An Audit Commission report (1996) published shortly before the 1997 Labour landslide, reviewing the arrangements provided for young offenders by public services, found, yet again, few examples of effective coordinating strategy in action. A strategy requires a framework, however. The report recommended that although local government already provided one such structure, local authority chief executives should initiate forums in which all relevant local authority services and other agencies participate. These should, in the context of children's services plans, develop strategies for addressing and preventing youth crime and should be translated into action at strategic, management and practitioner levels. Central government was asked to help 'by giving local authorities a duty to convene inter-agency groups [and] requiring other agencies a duty to co-operate with such groups' (Audit Commission 1996: para. 168). Finally, the Commission recommended coordination between government departments.

Factors contributing to successful inter-agency cooperation

In contrast to formal government reports, those from independent bodies and the voluntary sector focus more narrowly on particular groups of young people and possible solutions. They tend to be local and specific, ranging from small case studies to large-scale surveys. Many, supported by pressure group or other charitable endeavour, are driven by committed researchers with a tale to tell. As a result, they paint a picture somewhat closer to the realities of practitioner and client life than does the government report. Their usefulness lies in the attention they give to process, to the voice and experience of young people and to the front-line workers closest to them. The detailed examples they give, or practical suggestions they make, provide a useful accompaniment to the full-scale government report. Taken together, reports and legislation suggest a number of factors contributing to successful inter-agency working. Table 2.1 summarizes these and while there is much more that could have been added, the following factors are selected for consideration here.

Definitions of need

Conceptual difficulties over the use of terms such as children 'in need', 'at risk', 'learning difficulty' or 'special educational needs' have not been resolved. Children and young people have been categorized and compartmentalized in different ways by different agencies. The group most frequently studied and legislated for over the longest period are young offenders. More recently truants, the excluded, the abused, young carers and the homeless have received attention but there has been little recognition that the same young people are frequently to be found in more than one of these categories. Thus young people with multiple problems are the least well served by society, constantly on the move between different agencies and claiming their concern and resources. Many appear only to receive the attention of legislators and report writers because of their potential risk, and/or burden, to society, or because, as in the case of victims of abuse, claims for their need for support are made on the grounds of social conscience. Inter-agency cooperation tends to focus on subsets (young offenders, the homeless etc.) of the wider

Table 2.1 Inter-agency cooperation in transition

Factors Government	Before 1970 Con/Labour/Con	1971–1988 Con/Labour/Con	1989–1994 Conservative	After 1994 Con/Labour
Legislation	1963 and 1969 CYP Acts; Circular 10/64; 1970 Education Act; 1970 Local Authority Social Services Act	1973 Health Service Re-organisation Act; 1975 SDA; 1976 RRA; 1981 and 1988 Education Acts	1989 Children Act; 1993 Education Act; 1994 C.o.P.	1995 Disability Rights Act; 1997 Green Paper (Education); 1998 Action Programme (SEN); 2001 SEN and Disability Act
Values/ principles	Assimilation	Social justice; social welfare; equal opportunities	From needs to rights and the free market; entitlement	Market plus social justice; positive action; equity; 'joined up thinking'
Leadership/ commitment	Beveridge; Butler; Kilbrandon; Seebohm; Plowden; Barnardo's; Shelter	Court; Warnock; Fish; Swann; NCB; NSPCC	Butler-Sloss; Elton; Utting; Audit Commission; NCB; JRF; Save the Children	Audit Commission; NCB; JRF; CRDU; Young Minds; Children's Legal Centre; Social Exclusion Unit
Concepts and definitions	Segregation; child as object; categories	Special educational needs	Children in need/at risk; compartmentalism;	'Through the net'; 'at promise'; child as citizen; children's rights; self advocacy
Focus of interest	Young offenders; handicapped; maladjusted	Learning difficulties; SEN; in care; EBD; excluded; truants	As before plus abused; categories of learning and behavioural difficulty; homeless; carers	Young offenders; truants; excluded; looked after; early years; post-16

	Children's Hearing (Scotland)	Joint consultative committees (JCCs); Multiprofessional assessment (MPA)	Working together to safeguard children; Scottish Youth Strategy	Children's Services Plans
Structures	Children's Hearing (Scotland)	Joint consultative committees (JCCs); Multiprofessional assessment (MPA)	Working together to safeguard children; Scottish Youth Strategy	Children's Services Plans
Initiatives	Child Guidance	Intermediate treatment (IT)		Sure Start; Connexions
Terminology used to promote cooperation	Multi/inter-professional; collaborative/joint working	Collaboration/cooperation	Inter/multi-agency cooperation	Inter-agency/organizational coordination/collaboration/meta-strategy; collaborative advantage; networking; network broking; partnership
Agency strategies to promote cooperation	Teams; training in social work for doctors/health visitors	Multidisciplinary teams	Inter/multi-agency teams and projects	Inter-/intra-agency projects; inter-agency training; SEN Regional Partnerships
Resources	Available to service the Children's Panel (Scotland)	For statements of SEN	SEN	SEN; EBD via projects; Education Action Zones
Quantitative data	Young offenders	Isle of Wight Study (health); SEN	Young offenders/looked after	1995 OECD study (at risk children and youth); Young offenders/truancy

group of children and young people at risk, while no study, it appears, is specifically concerned with 'through the netness', though the concept is implied in some.

Joint training to develop jointly agreed definitions, terminology and procedures

Training emerged as a key factor promoting effective inter-agency work during the 1980s and 1990s. Plowden recommended, for example, an element of social work training in the training of doctors and health visitors. A decade later, Warnock emphasized training within the teaching profession, as well as inter-professional training. Training is identified in this study as an important factor because it can bring about the changes in attitude and behaviour needed to work across agency boundaries. It has been slow to develop, however, and still features only minimally in the initial training of practitioners (Lloyd 1998).

Needs and numbers

Quantitative data have been a significant factor underpinning successful inter-agency work. Much of the quantitative information which would concentrate agency minds on the extent and range of need has only been available relatively recently and still does not cover those who fall 'through the net'. In this instance, qualitative data on their own are insufficient, or too anecdotal or extreme, to support the claims of those who favour inter-agency coordinating structures as a strategy for improving the life chances of those who fall 'through the net'. If, agencies seem to be saying, inter-agency work is to be promoted, despite all the difficulties, then the case for it must be made out. 'Practitioners are often unwilling to leave the safety of their agencies, or risk current services to the majority, for the sake of a tiny minority. Thus justification for inter-agency work depends on the justification for it numerically' (Roaf 2001: 178), as many reports, from Kilbrandon (1964), through Warnock (1978) and the Audit Commission (1994, 1996) to the OECD (1995) affirm.

Resources

Although many of the government reports cited mention resource implications, legislation rarely does. The implication is that local providers will redistribute resources to meet the demands placed on them by the legislators. This has unfortunate consequences for other equally essential services at the local level. As an example, it was not foreseen that the detailed procedures put in place to cope with child protection would mean a transfer of resources and energy to this group and away from other vulnerable groups, such as young carers or homeless young people. Methods such as the ring fencing of money jointly held on behalf of agencies which can then be used flexibly to promote inter-agency practice are unusual, and often depend on private sector initiative. Studies of the costs to agencies and society of, for example, residential care, exclusion, juvenile crime or truancy continue to be, as Parsons *et al.* (1994) points out, a relatively new field. This approach is proving, however, to be an effective tool in analysing the relative merits of agency cooperation or the lack of it. Even when resources are, as in the case of special educational needs provision, 'indicated', they are as easily lost or misdirected as the young people themselves. Agencies find it hard to make the rapid readjustments and reprioritization that children at risk of falling 'through the net' require. Consequently, the evidence, from monitoring organizations such as the Audit Commission (1992a, 1994), of misuse of resources, delays and lack of accountability strengthens the case for inter-agency coordination.

Coordinating structures

Although legislation exhorts agencies to cooperate, over the period covered in this study, there have been few examples of structures or procedures to bring this about. Where these exist they have been set up in response to needs or crises of pressing concern at the time. Indeed, it is tempting to conclude that the main factor contributing to best practice is the discovery of some fresh abuse or difficulty sufficiently compelling to ensure a humanitarian response from a reasonable government. Too often it has been left to charitable trusts and local groups to take the initiative. Young offenders, disabled children and abused children were the main groups singled out for the attention of legislators in this respect. From reports relating to these groups we inherit the Scottish Children's Hearing, the multiprofessional assessment of children with special educational needs and the Child Protection Panel. Each has contributed to the development of effective inter-agency coordination and joined up action, demonstrating that legislation leading to inter-agency protocols can be effective. The 1981 Education Act, though influential, has had more success in promoting effective intra- rather than inter-agency work. The multiprofessional assessment never quite achieved that objective, being more of a 'paper' exercise than an example of active cooperation between practitioners. Turning to structures which do not compartmentalize young people, Scotland's Youth Strategy was set up in advance of the 1989 Children Act. It was followed ten years later by similar developments, mandatory only since 1997, in England and Wales. The significance of these initiatives in endorsing the importance of inter-agency cooperation at all levels has been incalculable.

Other aspects of government activity have also influenced the deep structures of how agencies go about their business. The restructuring of social services following Seebohm is one of these, the development of the comprehensive school and the move away from segregation towards integration, and now inclusion, of children with special educational needs is another (DfEE 1997). These initiatives have helped to break down, or readjust, boundaries, creating a climate in which protocols for active inter-agency cooperation can be developed. However, each agency must operate effectively itself before embarking on work with other agencies (Kendrick and Fraser 1993;

Parsons *et al.* 1994). Intra-agency work needs as much attention as inter-agency work and should precede it, with agencies ready to enforce existing legislation and support pressure groups promoting new legislation.

Conclusion

Inter-agency collaboration has been perceived to be part of the solution for an increasing range of problems over the past thirty years, but is only recently becoming the subject of research in its own right. Perhaps it is appropriate that more thought is given to this now, as the push to inclusion gives integrity to a wide range of matters that were previously boxed according to disciplinary and bureaucratic boundaries.

Policy-making on behalf of vulnerable young people seems to have been motivated as much for the benefit of society as a whole as for individual young people. Egalitarian concepts of social justice, inclusion and welfare thus run alongside more utilitarian concepts of community safety, the preservation of law and order and the upholding of traditional values. The reports leading to legislation acknowledge the potentially contentious nature of these issues but rarely set up the inter-agency structures that would coordinate inter-agency cooperation and facilitate joined up action in practice. Meanwhile, evidence from practitioner accounts suggests that lack of coordination presents difficulties for them at all levels in the agencies, affecting outcomes for their young clients.

Perhaps the lesson of Seebohm is the most significant. No matter how agencies group or regroup, the need for cooperation remains and without it clients are no more likely to receive a coordinated response from agencies than they were a generation ago. We need to go back to Seebohm, Kilbrandon, Plowden and Warnock and reinterpret them for the future. Seebohm's intention was for a team approach, Plowden's for a whole-community approach, Kilbrandon's for prevention and Warnock's for coordination. In every case, the reports recommending best practice, and policy guided by that, were superseded by legislation narrowed to something more simplistic. In the event, practitioners work in the rough marginal ground between ideal and reality, between report and legislation and best and worst practice. Children continue to be vulnerable in these circumstances, with little attention paid to their wishes and feelings or to their rights as citizens.

CHAPTER THREE

Agencies, practitioners and children

In this chapter the focus shifts from legislation and policy to agencies and practitioners. Moves towards increasing inter-professionalism, the idea of inter-agency work as a new area of specialist expertise and the development of inter-agency agencies are discussed in the context of changing concepts of childhood and adolescence.

Agencies

Primary care agencies in this country have their antecedents as public services in Victorian times. Although this period is now associated in the public mind with charitable motives and benefaction, this was not necessarily the case.

> the Victorians eschewed the charitable approach as being too sporadic and soft centred. In the construction of the major public services in which the professionals now ply their specialisms they were moved by harsher more earth bound motives.
>
> (Midwinter 1977: 104)

Self-interest then as now ordained the expediency of preventative work to avoid mass disease, with consequent loss of working hours leading to economic ruin nationally or, more cynically, for the ruling classes. John Ruskin, the Victorian moral philosopher, suggests that humanitarian motives need both agencies and an enabling legal framework.

> I hold it for indisputable that the first duty of a state is to see that every child born therein shall be well housed, clothed, fed and educated 'til it attain the years of discretion. But in order to the affecting of this, the

governments must have an authority over the people of which we do not
now so much as dream.

(Letter xiii, 21 March 1867; 1994 edition: 79)

Motive, in professional and agency development, whether utilitarian or
charitable, political or philanthropic, affects outcomes and mode of operation. A comment from Warnock (1978: para. 2.1) serves as a reminder of
the manner in which voluntary and state provision are thought to have
evolved:

> As with ordinary education, education for the handicapped began with
> individual and charitable enterprise. There followed in time the inter-
> vention of government, first to support voluntary effort and make good
> deficiencies through state provision, and finally to create a national
> framework in which public and voluntary agencies could act in partner-
> ship to see that all children, whatever their disability, received a suitable
> education.

Subsequent writers have found this analysis somewhat simplistic. Tomlinson
(1982: 7) quotes many examples to substantiate her claim that:

> special education did not develop because individuals or groups were
> inspired by benevolent humanitarianism to 'do good' to certain chil-
> dren. The idea that the development of special education was solely a
> matter of 'doing good' and was civilised progress can possibly be traced
> to eighteenth-century humanism and nineteenth-century Christian re-
> form. But humanitarianism can itself become an ideology legitimating
> principles of social control within society.

Warnock's description of the Charity Organisation Society is revealing.
Founded in 1869 to coordinate charity, its activities included campaigns for
special schools for the feeble minded (Warnock 1978: para. 2.18). Among
its patrons were those who had interests in the control of defective groups
and their separation from normal groups in the interest of social control. Thus
it would appear that if humanitarian ideals can be distorted within single
agencies, they could, in principle, become even more seriously distorted
through agency cooperation. Welton (1989: 21), examining the post-1988
Education Act framework of social policy, saw the 1981 Education Act on
Special Educational Needs as 'a survivor from the broader welfare project
which had its symbolic foundations in the Beveridge Report followed by
three decades of development in social legislation'. The immediate post-war
period under a Labour government, through the need for economic and
social reconstruction, brought to fruition principles which had been developing throughout the latter part of the nineteenth century. The Second
World War served to heighten awareness of the needs of the most vulnerable
in society, including children. However, the 1981 Act was not merely a
survivor of the previous welfare project. It was also a front runner in the
equal opportunities legislation which was part of the 1970s discourse on
social justice. If 'needs' could no longer be asserted through the welfare

project, as came to be the case during the 1980s, then rights would have to be demanded, ultimately through the courts.

More recently, discussing the distributional effects of the markets in education and notions of choice, equity and control, Gewirtz *et al.* (1995: 9) suggest that: 'Broadly speaking, the arguments of those on the right seem to be predicated on a desert-based definition of equity while those on the left appear to be using a needs-based definition.' Inevitably the relationship between agency and client is sensitive to the definitions used and the principles on which they are based: it is of little use to appeal to welfare needs in a society which only acknowledges rights.

For some philosophers (O'Neill 1986) the concept of need is a useful vehicle for bringing together those who assert rights and those bound by duty or obligation to fulfil them. Although the Tory government of the late 1980s did not feel bound by either duty or obligation to consider the special needs of individuals (the 1988 Act makes no mention of the principles of the 1981 Act), the 1989 Children Act reaffirms the previous welfare project, couched in the language of needs, obligations and duties. At a time of mounting disillusionment and alienation among public sector workers, the Children Act brought them together, thus contributing to a resurgence of interest in agency collaboration.

Definitions: agencies and inter-agency work

The development of inter-agency work is reflected in the vocabulary used to describe it, much of it confusing. 'Inter/multi-disciplinary', 'inter/multi-professional' and 'inter/multi-agency' are terms used somewhat loosely among practitioners, sometimes interchangeably. Writers on the subject have usually felt obliged to stake out their own claims for definition, as in, for example, Gyarmati (1986), or more recently, Lacey (2001). Parsloe (1981) notes a range of terms used to discuss the integration of services and relates these to sets of actions associated with key agency relationships, while pointing out the general lack of agreement over definition.

Huxham (1996), discussing relationships between public and non-profit organizations, uses a more extensive vocabulary than is to be found among child care agencies, with terms such as partnership, participation, inter- and cross-organizational, mixed sector. Furthermore, this vocabulary is applied to voluntary and community organizations, cooperation between groups and agencies, across the public and private sectors and among local authorities, government and business organizations. Local, national and international perspectives are also considered with words such as *alliance, bridge, network* and *coalition*, to distinguish between different forms of inter-organizational relationship. However, Huxham (1996: 240) comments:

> While such distinctions may have value in principle, there seems to be little consensus in the field about how the terms are used either in theory or practice, so they do not provide a consistent and helpful practice . . . In this article therefore, the term collaboration will be used to refer to all kinds of inter-organizational relationship.

From the evidence of a number of texts since the late 1970s, it seems that while the vocabulary being used in the discourse of inter-organizational collaboration is not new, definitions are still fluid. In fact, this heady mix of mainly Latin origin nouns and verbs used to elaborate the simple Anglo-Saxon derived term 'working together' is a remarkable feature of past and current literature on this subject.

Huxham and Macdonald (1992: 53) distinguish:

- *Collaboration*: when participants work together to pursue a meta-mission while also pursuing their individual missions.
- *Cooperation*: when organizations interact only so that each may achieve its own mission better.
- *Coordination*: in situations where there may be no direct interaction between organizations, but where an organization aims to ensure that its own activities take into account those of others.

In these terms, the development of local authority children's services plans, developed in response to the 1989 Children Act, would require the formulation of a shared *meta-strategy*, defined by Huxham and Macdonald (1992: 53) as:

> a statement of strategy for the collaboration, consisting of a *meta-mission* and *meta-objectives*. Such a statement will presumably be most useful where the collaborating organizations have a commitment to ends which are outside the direct remits of any of them. Though it is by no means impossible that this could occur in the private sector, it seems much more likely to be the case in the public or voluntary sectors.

In formulating these definitions these writers emphasize the 'need to pay deliberate attention to developing collaborative relationships' (p. 53). In their view the notion of meta-strategy distinguishes between what individual organizations can do on their own and what can only be achieved through collaboration. By contrast to the literature examined in Chapter 2, in which inter-agency cooperation was construed in terms of problems, studies across a wider range of organizations seem to have led to the development of a rich vocabulary expressing a variety of relationships stemming from proactive solution-focused approaches to collaboration.

Given the breadth of activity undertaken by the statutory agencies involved with the care of children, inter-agency activity goes far beyond multi/inter-disciplinary or multi/inter-professional activity. It is concerned with the manner in which each agency operates as a whole at the levels of both policy and practice. It is also concerned with the operation of these agencies at national as well as local levels and with their links with the voluntary sector.

Agency purpose

In general terms agency purpose consists of a core of responsibilities, translated in a range of services decreed by government and tradition. The exact nature of the brief is an evolving one and in some instances arbitrary. In the case of children and young people, the agencies concerned, in addition to health, education and social services, could include probation, police, housing, employment and transport. In some cases their services overlap. For example, the questions of who pays for transport to school or hospital, who funds speech therapy and who employs education social workers or youth workers have been, and continue to be, matters for dispute and, in some cases, litigation. Professionals trained in a number of disciplines can find employment in a range of statutory and non-statutory agencies involved with children. The ease with which they can cross agency boundaries is, in reality, a matter of how the agencies concerned choose to interpret their purpose and these interpretations vary between and within countries. Norway, for example, has a tradition of school as a key support to families. 'Once a child enters school, it is the teacher who is relied upon to work most closely with the parents to promote the child's welfare . . . educators ideally serve as the human link between families and other services available at the municipal level' (Hagen and Tibbitts 1994: 21). This tradition arose in a country characterized by a strong commitment to child-centred policies and to equality of opportunity and outcome.

Services thus develop and become differentiated over time in response to a range of political, organizational and societal needs. Each one, as it develops, gradually enters the mainstream or 'core mission' of the agency concerned, complete with an entourage of employees. These individuals then develop, through a combination of internal agency culture, management and pay structures, a loyalty to the agency employing them.

Agency strategies promoting a more flexible response to client needs and allowing for rapid reprioritization have been slow to develop. From their work with people involved in inter-organizational collaboration, Huxham and Vangen (1996) identify two broad themes: those concerning agency goals and priorities, and those concerning the manner in which these expressions of purpose are communicated. Ultimately, the dilemma for agencies centres on how they prioritize the marginal at the expense of the core, the risky at the expense of the routine. To resolve this, inter-agency work has to prove that successful work with the marginal and risky can bring improvements for all. The key question becomes how to secure collaborative advantage, defined by Huxham (1996: 241) as happening when 'something unusually creative is produced – perhaps an objective is met – that no organization could have produced on its own and when each organization, through collaboration, is able to achieve its own objectives better than it could alone'.

How, then, do agencies first identify and recognize the significance of marginalized young people, among whom are some of the most vulnerable young people in society? Second, having identified them, how do they transfer them from the margin to the core of agency responsibility? What factors distort or deflect agency purpose in this respect? It seems probable that if agencies were to focus more closely on the margin, a natural consequence would be to see collaboration as a central agency activity rather than one which is marginal. This reversal of the usual emphasis would counterbalance the general tendency of agencies to marginalize those whose needs might oblige them to depart from traditional ways of working. In recent work this trend has been noted (Glenny 2001), adding strength to the view that it is problems that are 'through the net', not people.

Factors influencing inter-agency work with children and young people

A number of factors are regularly put forward to explain the difficulties agencies have in working together. The problem has a long history and the same litany features in almost every study. Mapstone's pioneering study of services contributing to the mental health of children notes that the conflict between agency approaches was compounded by:

> organisational fragmentation (in particular, separate budgets, different administrative hierarchies, procedures and priorities and employment of the various administrative and professional staff to different authorities and agencies) can defeat the best intentions of those involved in providing mental health services to children and young people.
>
> (Mapstone 1983: 92)

Since the 1980s this list has been added to by factors such as the speed of legislative change, local government reorganisation, the introduction of the market into human service provision and an increased demand for accountability, all accompanied by increases in bureaucratic intervention.

Other writers emphasize the 'moral agenda of social reconstruction in a "societyless society"' (Welton 1989: 26), which in itself has increased anxiety levels already raised by financial constraints, job losses and legislative change. In Scotland concerns were expressed that changes in local government administrative boundaries might constrain agencies previously willing to collaborate (Kendrick et al. 1996).

Even while extolling the benefits of collaboration, others draw attention to its difficulties. Mawhinney (1994: 43), arguing for ecological perspectives on collaboration, cautions against too facile assumptions that:

> collaboration will result in more efficient and effective services for the public. Yet, if past efforts at co-operation are taken into account, it is evident that sustained collaboration will raise problems of communication, control and power . . . Moreover, if the purpose of collaboration is to better serve the needs of 'at risk' children and youth, then a major underlying cause of risk, that is poverty, cannot be ignored. Co-ordination or even collaboration cannot overcome poverty, nor will they resolve all the problems of fragile families.

Likewise, despite their enthusiasm for collaboration, Huxham and Macdonald (1992) also caution that there is a fine balance to be struck between gaining the benefits of collaborating and making the situation worse. There is also the question of resources: 'costing the benefits of collaboration will, of course, be difficult, but some kind of weighing up process is necessary to ensure that the costs do not far exceed the benefits – or conversely that the benefits are recognised as outweighing the costs' (p. 52).

Thus the potential pitfalls can result in a degree of agency inertia with respect to inter-agency collaboration. Huxham (1996: 239) finds that:

> the rhetoric surrounding inter-organisational relationships is so positive, emphasizing mutual benefit through co-operation and partnership, that those involved seem often to be taken by surprise when difficulties surface because they have had no warning that they have entered complex territory.

For Huxham, the term 'collaborative inertia' describes the situation when the progress of a group set up to achieve 'collaborative advantage' slows down compared to what a casual observer might expect it to achieve. Huxham's experience of this phenomenon led to an exploration of the management of relationships across organisational boundaries. She concludes that collaborative situations are inherently complex: 'there are no easy prescriptive guidelines, but . . . sensitivity to the areas of difficulty and to the ways in which they can be minimized is essential' (Huxham 1996: 240). These she identifies as:

- multiple, often hidden, goals;
- differences in professional language, culture and procedures;
- incompatible collaborative capability;
- perceived power imbalances but no authority hierarchy;
- the tension between autonomy and accountability;
- time involved in managing logistics.

These are balanced by success factors. Huxham cites Mattessich and Monsey's (1992) compilation of these:

- mutual respect, understanding and trust;
- appropriate cross-section of members;
- open and frequent communication;
- sufficient funds;
- skilled convenor;
- members see collaboration as in their self-interest;
- history of collaboration or cooperation in the community;
- members share a stake in both process and outcome;
- multiple layers of decision-making;
- established informal and formal communication links;
- concrete attainable goals and objectives;
- shared vision;
- flexibility;
- development of clear roles and policy guidelines;
- collaborative group seen as leader in the community;
- political/social climate favourable;
- ability to compromise;
- adaptability;
- unique purpose.

Huxham points out that in all collaborative situations there is an inevitable tension between these sets of factors. Developing a shared vision, for example, might require some masking of goals, at least initially. There may also be mistaken beliefs about the ability of collaboration to reduce costs to each partner in the collaboration. This is regarded by Huxham (1996: 241) as questionable:

> experience suggests that successful collaboration is highly resource intensive. Nevertheless, our own perspective on the value that can be aimed for in collaboration sets, in some respects, a much more demanding expectation. Rather than focusing on particular forms of benefit, we simply pose the question, 'how can advantage be gained by collaborating?'

If the point of collaboration is to achieve something important that can only be achieved that way, and shortage of money is a major agency constraint, then a clear logic to back the purpose of collaboration is an important prerequisite.

Studies such as Parsons *et al.* (1994) and Kendrick *et al.* (1996), complemented by statistics available from organizations such as the National Youth Agency, suggest that the cost to society caused by neglect of those at the margins of agency responsibility is so great as to be damaging to everyone. The lesson for agencies in this situation is that to neglect the marginal is to lose an opportunity to think creatively about strategies which ultimately benefit everyone. Developing meta-strategy to secure collaborative advantage in relation to this group is therefore of central importance to the way the agencies function for all. This might suggest that every effort should be made to ensure that *intra*-agency coordination functions so well that high-quality, expensive *inter*-agency work can be reserved for work which can only be achieved in that way. Alternatively, since children are, in general, a marginalized group, services for them should be part of a single fully coordinated inter-agency structure. Debates of this kind lie behind proposals for greater coordination of services for children between government departments (Audit Commission 1996, 1998; Hodgkin and Newell 1996; Newell 2000).

Professionals and inter-professionalism

Agencies are staffed by individuals whose personal and professional needs and aspirations interact closely with agency purpose and, to a large extent, determine its outcome. Factors influencing professionals towards or away from collaboration are therefore closely related to those influencing agencies. During the 1980s, the way in which professional training ensures the acquisition of particular values, expertise and identity was much debated. These values effectively mark the professional and tend to emphasize rather than blur professional boundaries which are later overlain and strengthened by agency boundaries. For Jaques (1986: 3), 'The boundaries are further reinforced by differences in methods of training, supervision and lifestyle, as well as the various habits of dress and behaviour that students develop as they model themselves on their professional mentors.'

Similarly, Bines (1992: 126) found 'considerable potential for conflict and territoriality, especially since the history and development of the professions has largely been based on securing status through exclusive knowledge and occupation demarcation'. Pilkington (1993), writing of Arnold *et al.*'s (1993) study of housing and community care in Oxfordshire, notes, as an added difficulty, a distinction between 'caring' and other agencies:

> poor housing, ill health and unmet care needs were inextricably linked. Yet the agencies persisted in responding to this mixture by acting uni-laterally. Rarely were demands for care and accommodation considered jointly; in some cases housing departments appeared openly reluctant to seek the support of other agencies. This was not a case of simple bloody-mindedness, but of dogged demarcation between professions. Housing officials saw themselves as separate from the caring services, and vice versa.
>
> (Pilkington 1993: 6)

The Thamesmead Interdisciplinary Project uncovered three main categories of expectation when professionals from different disciplines were brought together for training. These were:

- Cognitive: overcoming problems, exploding and creating myths, per-ceiving roles.
- Practice: discussion, role play, participation . . .
- Affective: 'alarming, but exciting', 'feeling slightly coerced', 'hope not going to be dominated by health visitors', 'many people will feel threatened'.

> (Higgins and Jaques 1986: 14)

Feelings of insecurity thus appear to underlie inter-agency and inter-professional relations, affecting the ability of individuals both to separate and to integrate the personal and professional in their working relationships. Whether staff work closely or separately across agency and professional boundaries depends too often on the personalities involved.

In the context of Huxham and Macdonald's (1992) discussion of collaborat-ive advantage, it is suggested here that if meta-strategy and a sense of meta-mission is required to promote collaboration, meta-cognitive abilities among the participants are also required. These abilities do not appear, from the evidence of inter-agency projects and reports, to be associated intrinsically with any particular professional skill or status, but to centre instead on well developed interpersonal skills.

Education, health and social services are exhorted, in much of the legisla-tion, to collaborate over the heads, so to speak, of the strongly demarcated professions within and among them. At the same time, a strong sense of professional values, identity and skill is required by client and agency. An expansion of interprofessional education and research is particulary needed to help lower the barriers between one profession and another, between academic and practitioner, and between expressions of what clients want and what they are considered by the professionals to need.

Nonetheless, a necessary tension exists between society's need for increasingly high levels of specialist professional expertise and individual consumers' or clients' need for a holistic, accessible service. This requires, as noted above, a response from the professions. They are, it is suggested here, likely to gain their most useful insights as to how to resolve these tensions from among their most vulnerable clients on the margins.

Factors standing in the way of effective interprofessional practice: necessary and unnecessary constraints

According to Gardner (1993: 262), 'It is constraints that make possible genuine achievements, including human innovation and creativity. In the absence of constraints, where all is theoretically possible, it would not be possible to make and recognize advances.' Gardner considers that 'the existence of constraints in human thought make possible . . . the cherished moments when humans overcome a prejudice, a bias, an entrenched way of thinking' (p. 262). Disciplines, he declares, are organized sets of constraints. He sees the fact that they advance and are transformed as proof that these constraints can be freeing as well as limiting. In relation to the disciplinary expert, he considers that the term 'constraints' may seem inappropriate:

> After all, in some ways, experts are empowered to overcome constraints, to stretch their skills and concepts in new and unanticipated directions. This state of enablement, however, is possible only because of a mastery that has been obtained, often quite painstakingly, over a number of years.
>
> (Gardner 1993: 8)

Gardner suggests that when individuals or groups confront what they consider to be a limit, openings or new configurations appear. One possible way of construing the development of professionalism over the past half-century is to see it as a series of confrontations with constraints of various kinds. Distinguishing between necessary and unnecessary constraints then assumes great significance. As an example, Gardner describes schools as bureaucratic institutions within communities subject to powerful pressures from, for example, legislation, the public, and professional organizations. It can therefore be difficult for schools to 'balance and integrate the mission of the school with the practices of the wider community' (p. 139). Knapp *et al.* (1994: 139), in an article on university-based preparation for collaborative interprofessional practice, accept the need for both specialist professional skills and inter-professionalism.

> Given that disciplines exist, in part to distinguish areas of special expertise from one another, it is natural that there should arise separate – and often competing – service philosophies . . . On the other hand, in the

world where professionals do their work as teachers, nurses, social workers, therapists, or administrators, they are confronted by challenges that are non-specific, that are related to whole individuals, complex families and communities. At a minimum, these challenges invite and often require co-operation or co-ordination among educational, health and social services.

Knapp *et al.* found that, on the whole, although barriers stood in the way of collaborative instruction and the development of a curriculum transcending disciplinary boundaries, 'Most of the barriers . . . appear to be passive, involving a lack of specific incentives to collaborate, rather than active opposition' (p. 140). Examples of three such barriers – confidentiality, professional jealousy and inertia – are considered next.

Confidentiality is frequently cited as one of the potential stumbling blocks to collaboration between professionals (Warnock 1978; Fish 1985). This appears to be especially marked in relation to professionals working with children. Confidentiality raises subtle questions about professional ethics, traditions and etiquette. However, it can also be used as an excuse to cover agency inertia and vested interests in maintaining the status quo. In this respect confidentiality can be a good example of an unnecessary constraint. Kadel and Routh (1994: 126) found that 'record sharing among service providers is usually necessary for providing co-ordinated services to families, but most agencies have confidentiality policies which restrict access to records'. Their strategy was to obtain parental consent to share information between agencies. Since parental consent was required anyway to obtain access to any service, this permission could be sought at the same time. Other strategies were to maintain limited access to highly confidential information (such as mental health treatment) but to include broad statements about referral and recommendations in central files that are accessible to parents and practitioners, to give access to records by those who had sworn an oath of confidentiality and to reconsider the regulations as part of new coordinated record-keeping systems.

The Cleveland Report (Butler-Sloss 1988) raised the issue of confidentiality and information sharing in the area of child abuse. Subsequent government guidance on the conduct of inter-agency work in relation to child protection established two important principles:

Ethical and statutory codes concerned with confidentiality and data protection are not intended to prevent the exchange of information between professional staff who have a responsibility for ensuring the protection of children.

In child protection work the degree of confidentiality will be governed by the need to protect the child. Social workers and others working with a child and the family must make clear to those providing information that confidentiality may not be maintained if the withholding of information will prejudice the welfare of the child.

(DoH/DES and Welsh Office 1991)

Warnock (1978: para. 16.17) linked confidentiality to the development of trust between professionals:

> guidelines and codes of practice on the sharing of information cannot be a substitute for personal knowledge on the part of individuals of their professional colleagues who are also concerned with meeting a particular child's needs and appreciation of their colleagues' professional expertise. Indeed without such personal knowledge and trust it is unlikely that any exchange of information will be as useful as is possible.

In the case of *professional jealousy*, Kadel and Routh (1994) suggest that 'turf' issues in inter-professional practice arise from, for example, fear of job losses, funding limitations or uncertainty over breaking new ground. This is an important factor where children and young people are involved, since challenges to agencies are continually being presented by clients who are not the exclusive responsibility of any one agency; for example, young people bereaved, pregnant or acting as carers. Accounts of inter-agency projects suggest that agency attitudes towards 'through the net' adults and 'through the net' children differ (Vagg 1987; Lloyd 1994). The former have few champions and no 'Ah' factor, and agencies are more willing to relinquish responsibility to another agency or inter-agency group. By contrast, practitioners sometimes have difficulty giving up responsibility for a child even where this would be helpful, rather than suffer the opprobrium of relinquishing it. To do so would appear to constitute a personal affront or, worse still, a dereliction of duty. This is reinforced by public opinion, in the subtle differences in attitude towards professionals involved with neglected children compared to those involved with neglected adults. Professional jealousy may also be a factor inhibiting collaboration when professionals within agencies share case loads with others of lower status or working at their agency margin.

Finally, on the subject of *inertia*, according to Weatherley and Lipsky (1977: 172), 'street level bureaucrats' – that is, public employees who interact with the public and make decisions calling for individual initiatives and routines – 'have substantial discretion in the execution of their work.' These are often middle managers squeezed by the need of their superiors to delegate authority, their own need to maintain credibility and accountability as middle managers and the demands of their clients. For them it becomes professionally almost unthinkable to do otherwise than make the system cope, whatever the demands. In exceptional cases this can result in innovation, but too often 'bureaucratic coping behaviours cannot be eliminated' (p. 196). Although originally observed in the 1970s, the same phenomenon still exists: 'Community Care's original premise – that individuals' desires and needs come first – has become partially obscured under a mountain of bureaucratic inertia and inadequate resources' (Arnold *et al.* 1993).

Bowman (1990: 108) sees symptoms sometimes described as 'inertia' in terms of 'momentum' – 'Organisations have a strong tendency to continue doing what they have done in the past' – thus introducing a more dynamic quality to the concept. Inter-agency work, for example, is a field associated with innovation and risk-taking. Participants can become used to being involved with the new and the creative. This provides a motivating factor in their work at the expense of the need for stability, and a settling to longer-term strategy and more permanent inter-agency relationships once the desired innovation has been achieved. It is not yet known how inter-agency innovators will manage in such circumstances.

Brooks and Bate (1994: 181), in their study of agency reaction to impending change, consider that a number of features of agency culture can combine to cause not simply actively negative responses, but 'an indifference to change at the local level – indifference on the grand scale'. Even though people knew about the change and could talk about it, they lacked practical understanding of it and it seemed irrelevant. In a related context, Adler (1994: 10) points out: 'Organizations can constrain or enable interorganizational efforts, but collaboration is a person-to-person activity. Thus interpersonal ties are critical to the success of interorganizational relationships.' Adler quotes comments at a meeting of the Centre for Collaboration for Children which draw attention to the paradox between the need for interpersonal ties and resistance to change. This was the importance of the 'B team'. These are people in organizations who tell reformers: 'I've *been* here *be*fore you came and I'll *be* here after you go!' (p. 10).

Developing interprofessional competencies

For Knapp *et al.* (1994: 138), most definitions of the trained professional 'do not reflect the competencies we know to be associated with interprofessional collaborative practice.' The Training for Interprofessional Collaboration (TIC) project showed that standards defining what beginning social workers should know were fairly specific about collaborative skills. Teachers, however, with the exception of those training for special education, made no reference to these skills.

A fundamental task for TIC was to develop some consensus 'around the common professional domain which is the focus of interprofessional work' (p. 143). Definitions, they found, were required for the key terms 'competence', 'collaboration' and 'practitioner'. They quote Fenichel and Eggbeer's (1990) definition of 'competence' as 'the ability to do the right thing at the right time, for the right reasons' (Knapp *et al.* 1994: 143). They expand this by proposing that competence:

> involves the capacity to analyze a situation, consider alternative approaches, select and skilfully apply the best observation or intervention techniques, evaluate the outcome, and articulate the rationale for each step of the process. Competence generally requires a combination of knowledge, skills, and experience. Competence for work with children and families cannot be inferred from the completion of academic coursework alone; it must be demonstrated.
>
> (p. 143)

Interprofessional collaboration in human service delivery they define as:

an interactive process through which individuals and organizations with diverse expertise, experience and resources join forces to plan, generate, and execute solutions to mutually identified problems related to the welfare of families and children.

(p. 140)

TIC organized competencies into five domains: intrapersonal, interpersonal, group, organizational and sociocultural. It found, however, that 'what collaborating practitioners needed to know and know how to do could not be disaggregated neatly, but rather combined knowledge, skills and attitudes within the five domains' (p. 144). If, as its assessment suggested, collaborative competence was in part a matter of personal flexibility and openness to ideas, could this, the project leaders asked, be taught?

While learning activities could be arranged that would highlight the importance of being flexible, encourage students to approach a problem flexibly, and even model flexible behaviour, there was no guarantee that the message would get through to individuals with certain types of personalities.

(p. 144)

Kadel and Routh (1994: 129) note that the challenge for practitioners in the implementation of collaboration is a dual one affecting organizations and participants. 'Participants in reform must also consider the total set of goals involved in an innovation and need to realize that collaboration is just one of many ongoing changes in an organization.' According to Fullan (1992), leaders capable of building collaborative work cultures should be enablers rather than finders of solutions. They should help to build a vision among participants, employ conflict resolution strategies, encourage collegiality and respect for individuals and provide ongoing professional development of practitioners. Since leadership skills are almost certain to be required in the implementation process these should also be included in core competencies for collaboration.

Returning to the ideas of Huxham and Macdonald (1992) and Huxham (1996) on 'collaborative ability', it seems that the competencies required for inter-professional collaboration crystallize around the notion of 'the ability to do the right thing, at the right time, for the right reasons.' This appears to be the key ability needed to develop meta-strategy and, when analysed, amounts to meta-cognitive abilities of some complexity.

Taken together, these ideas suggest that the competencies required of inter-agency collaborators are encapsulated in Gardner's (1993: 240) definition of interpersonal intelligence:

the ability to notice and make distinctions among other individuals and, in particular, among their moods, temperaments, motivations and intentions ... Interpersonal knowledge permits a skilled adult to read the intentions and desires – even when these have been hidden – of many other individuals and, potentially, to act upon this knowledge – for example, by influencing a group of disparate individuals to behave along desired lines.

According to Mitchell and Scott (1994: 77), 'Only if staff professionalism is characterised by focused engagement as well as skilful intervention will real needs be addressed.' Today, professionalism goes beyond specialized expertise, with knowledge of the process of collaboration entering the core knowledge new professionals acquire (Knapp *et al.* 1994). The literature suggests that interest in inter-organizational collaboration, whether in the world of commerce or in human services, is a growing field of academic and practical interest. This can be accounted for partly by increasing global interdependence and ease of communication, but also by the importance now attached to inter-personal skills in daily life. These, in turn, are a natural consequence of developments in psychological theory since the 1950s, coupled with a relaxation of traditional class and other social barriers. In terms of communication at least, a more egalitarian lifestyle and the accountability of public services to the consumer play a part. Clients expect professionals to cooperate on their behalf and this has been a challenge readily accepted by those with well-developed interpersonal skills. Thus the language of exhortation used by report writers and legislators to promote collaboration is pushing at an open door. The question now is how to channel this intelligence in a manner which will benefit children.

Children and young people

Inter-agency work as a new professionalism, a concept still viewed with suspicion despite increasing numbers working in this field and a growing literature, is developing at a time when agency and public perceptions of children and young people are changing rapidly. How are young people reacting to changes in their status, rights and responsibilities? How are practitioners developing their advocacy role to create human services operating not for their own benefit, but in the interests of the client? As clients, children and young people have needs not only as members of families, but on their own account as rights-bearing citizens. The tension continues between protecting children and protecting their rights.

Conceptions of childhood

Studies undertaken through the 1990s (for example, Kumar 1993; Kempson 1996) detail the changes in living conditions of, and attitudes to, women and children in recent years. The effect has been to add juvenilization to the already well documented feminization of poverty. Children, as Holtermann (1996) points out, fare disproportionately badly because their general environment is poor through exposure to, for example, health risks, pollution and danger on the roads. Many cannot, through poverty, access the advantages better off children are gaining.

A number of factors contribute to this: lack of child care facilities, the speed at which children grow up and mature and the increased risks they are exposed to. In general, many of today's children have more freedom and more opportunities than formerly, but some have much less. Researchers note continued concern about issues such as illegal child labour, young homelessness, youth crime and exclusion from school (Graham and Bowling 1995; Hyams-Parish 1996). Many children reaching adolescence in the new millennium have to shoulder the risks and responsibilities of adults both at work and at home. In addition, those most exposed to adult risks are often accorded least status, with least knowledge of their rights.

The New Right project of the 1980s and 1990s contributed to this state of affairs, by putting the clock back on an earlier philosophy emphasizing the importance of preventative work, nurture and universal provision. Young people then were seen as in need of care, not control, and treatment, not punishment. Child Guidance and the comprehensive school movement of the 1960s and 1970s reinforced the idea that there was a continuum of need, while courts at the time could offer, through Intermediate Treatment, a range of therapeutic approaches to the problem of juvenile crime. During the 1970s this was given added weight by the passing of anti-discrimination legislation in relation to minority ethnic groups, women and children with disabilities. Inclusion and the notion of children's rights became more clearly articulated, through, for example, the raising of the school leaving age, the lowering of the age of majority, the campaign to end corporal punishment in school (NUT 1984) and the Gillick judgement (Lee 1986). By the time of Cleveland and the 1989 Children Act the rhetoric of children's rights was well developed. Shifts in attitude among adults and young people themselves have had an important effect on the way in which young people's needs are defined, by themselves, their families and the agencies involved.

Adolescence

The nature and concept of childhood and of adolescence have been variously understood throughout history and across all cultures. Expectations of, and attitudes towards, children and young people in the UK continue to be confused, as can be observed in media debates over substance abuse, the use of sanctions, forms of punishment, age of consent for marriage, employment, sex education, access to services and many other areas affecting the daily lives of young people, including the advice they are given.

These ambiguities centre on the confusion in society as to when and in what circumstances it is children or their rights which need protection. In the period leading to the implementation of the 1989 Children Act, workers in the primary care agencies considered that 'society has not decided whether teenagers are adults or children and there is a wide conflict of opinion as to "best practice"' (OCVA 1991: 10). Confusion among adults about adolescent needs, status and rights is likewise reflected in, for example, the definitions used in legislation such as the 1981 Education Act, the 1989 Children Act and the 1991 Criminal Justice Act. These contradictions are perpetuated in legislation affecting single agencies, such as the 1988 and 1993 Education Acts, and live on in key documents such as the revised SEN Code of Practice (DfES 2001c). A common definition would have been an obvious starting point and prerequisite for effective inter-agency practice.

While traditional theories of adolescence have been either psychoanalytic or sociological, as Coleman (1993) points out, a theory of normality is needed, rather than the theory of abnormality posed by traditional approaches. The evidence from case studies, and from autobiographies and life histories, serves as a caution against making any assumptions as to what can or cannot be done by, and to, adolescents and what they can achieve without any of the support networks normally considered essential. Agencies tend to have clearly defined objectives and legal responsibilities in relation to young people. However necessary, these may prevent them from responding quickly and flexibly, not only to social trends but also to the challenge inherent in working with the psychological and sociological volatility that characterizes adolescence.

Nonetheless, children have benefited from, and contributed to, the more holistic agency approaches to their care and education developed during the past decade. Pressure group and research activity has produced a climate in which the voice of the child can be heard (Clough and Barton 1995; Davie et al. 1996; Lewis and Lindsay 2000). However, children and young people present particular challenges to professionals. First, children challenge agency purpose and values because of their vulnerability, subordination and dependence, not only as members of oppressed minority groups, which many of them are, but because they are themselves minors (Boyden and Hudson 1985). Second, they challenge the interpersonal skills of practitioners, since they require practitioners to communicate with them in language appropriate to their age and understanding. Third, they challenge agency and practitioner commitment of time, energy and flexibility in the provision of resources, since their needs are personal and idiosyncratic. Finally, children challenge agencies and practitioners to cooperate, since a significant number require the services of more than one agency.

The development of 'inter-agency agencies' for children and families

The case for a single multifaceted agency for children has been argued for a long time. Before the reorganization of the personal social services in 1970 in England and Wales, children's officers played a significant role in their communities even though the framework within which they worked and accessed resources was fragmented (Seebohm 1968). Bronfenbrenner, Seebohm's contemporary, discussing the framework involved in the socialization of children, notes that the problems faced by children are rooted in the community:

> it is a sobering fact that, neither in our communities nor in the nation as a whole, is there a single agency that is charged with the responsibility of assessing or improving the situation of the child in his total environment. As it stands, the needs of children are parcelled out among a hopeless confusion of agencies . . . no one . . . is concerned with the total pattern of life for children in the community.
>
> (Bronfenbrenner 1970: 163)

Bronfenbrenner, one of the founder members of the Head Start programme in the United States in the 1960s, recommended the setting up of a Children's Commission. Similarly, in Norway there have been attempts in the past to use the school as an integrating agency in the care of children, a system now giving way as teacher workloads increase (Hagen and Tibbitts 1994).

In a study focusing specifically on programmes for collaboration between school and social services agencies in California, Mitchell and Scott (1994: 89) draw some conclusions which are of general significance. They consider that:

> The single most potent threat to successful interagency collaboration lies in the historical division of client needs into distinctive 'problems'... Once service agencies have been assigned unique responsibility for dealing with particular sets of client problems, the stage is set for systemic failure... As a result, client needs come to be defined in terms of an agency's capacity to respond.

From this follows the importance of reframing service responsibilities in terms of locality and administrative areas rather than client problems. In this respect, models of inter-agency collaboration involving the development of local networks are significant. Knapp et al. (1994) quote examples in the USA, such as the 30-agency network developed in Seattle, geographically located in a school district and supported by the city government and the Cities in School programme, the Philadelphia Children's Network and the Networking Committee of 30 agencies in Decatur, Georgia, formed as a community collaborative council. In the United Kingdom, Lloyd (1994) discusses the impact on local inter-agency collaboration of the 70-strong Oxford Adolescent Network (see Chapter 4).

For Mitchell and Scott (1994) the key issue here is the tension between, in their terms, case structured and programme structured work. This is the classic tension between 'upstream' and 'downstream',[1] between the individualized, needs-led, therapeutic interventions and 'whole-school' or community, issues-led, preventative measures. They cite the problems this tension causes in schools, particularly apparent when schools attempt to case manage large numbers of children rather than develop the ability to 'transcend traditional casework approaches in favor of holistic programs of family support (p. 89)'.

> In sum, interagency collaboration is supported when institutional norms allow geographic service regions to replace social problem-defining agency roles. This support is strengthened when these geographic centres establish an effective integration of program- and case-structured service planning, and when information systems provide documentation of service impact as well as guidance for service planning.
>
> (Mitchell and Scott 1994: 90)

Although practitioners are apt to caution against establishing a new layer of bureaucracy through the development of inter-agency agencies, others question the grounds of professional disquiet about this in terms of vested interests and barriers to collaboration. Hodgkin and Newell (1996), in a worldwide study of effective government structures for children, summarize the arguments for and against the development of such structures. In their report, published a year before local authority children's services plans became mandatory in England and Wales, they found that:

> Children's interests are dealt with by at least 14 government departments, each of which is dedicated, quite reasonably to the pursuit of excellence in its own sphere . . . but without carefully designed government structures and a commitment to forge the necessary connections between these separate responsibilities, the excellence the departments pursue may elude them or be thwarted by other's policies . . . Developing a children's perspective, and ensuring the impact of policies on children is appropriately considered throughout government, demands additional structures as well as a new political will.
>
> (p. 38)

Between top-down (ministers/commissioners for children) and bottom-up (local networks) strategies lies a range of inter-agency collaborative activity currently on a continuum from fully fledged agency to small project. However, even in the current climate of government support for joint working, it seems that government nationally and locally is easily confused by the immensity of the task of supporting children and families. Not only is it complex in itself on account of the number of agencies and professionals involved – 27 to support one child quoted by Lacey and Lomas (1993) – but debate continues over children's needs and rights, and the relative merits of intra- and inter-agency coordination, and upstream and downstream work.

Children and young people 'at risk'

This section considers some of the ways in which those considered to be 'through the net', 'in need' or 'at risk' are defined. Metaphors such as 'through the net', 'falling between stools, or cracks', 'falling between frameworks of care' and 'hot potatoes' are commonly used by agencies to describe those whose needs challenge them. They seem to have developed in association with metaphors such as 'seamless web' and 'welfare network' and to have entered common parlance in the late 1960s and 1970s. These metaphors are framed, with agencies construed as 'containers' (Lackoff and Johnson 1981) and clients as fugitives, or possessions: volatile, elusive, to be held or caught, sometimes as in a game, more generally with the risk of being dropped and lost. Definitions of this client group are hard to find.

A study in the mid-1980s of 'difficult to place' (DTP – a phrase virtually synonymous with TTN) adults records only one other report concerned with these people and this looked at them as patients (Vagg 1987). Brighton Health Authority defined the typical DTP patient as:

> a mentally abnormal individual, who exhibits behavioural, social and/or personality defects, who is likely to be known to multiple agencies

including the police and the courts, and who has a history of repeated rejections from various types of statutory and voluntary accommodation.
(Vagg 1987: 5)

Vagg's study refers to two definitions. These are:

those people who are seen to be misplaced by those at present attempting to contain them because of their bizarre and/or disruptive behaviour and who need accommodation providing a high level of tolerance and specialized assistance.

those for whom the statutory services find some difficulty in accepting responsibility because they have a need for a wide variety of support or provision which cannot be met by one service alone.

(p. 1)

He comments that the definitions can be criticized, since:

first, they identify by reference to potential solutions as well as problems, and secondly, they describe a group who may have little in common other than the fact that staff in various institutions find them difficult to cope with and difficult to do anything for.

(p. 1)

He concedes, however, that the term DTP has some usefulness in that it marks agencies' concern about those they seem unable to help, and that even though it centres on the bizarre and disruptive it is clear that other groups are also DTP. Vagg stresses that:

the label DTP applies to practitioner's assessments of the problems and needs of individuals in relation to the facilities they can offer; it is a description of a relationship, not an individual. Moreover, since that relationship is in large part defined by the objectives of the facilities dealing with them, there is no a priori guarantee that DTP people have any characteristics in common or that, in any strict sense, they constitute a 'group'.

(p. 17)

This adds another distinction to the one already noted between solution- and problem-based definitions. If agencies are to be persuaded to take the issues of 'through the netness' seriously they must be convinced that a significant number of people are affected. However, as Vagg found in his study, acquiring this information relies upon the assessments of the agencies as to who is or is not 'through the net' (TTN), yet agencies have different interpretations of who is DTP/TTN and there are no objective guidelines. Vagg saw this as a strength enabling the researcher to investigate and assess the conditions which agencies find difficult. He also noted instances in which agency opinion about the same client varied. In some, for example, only one agency found the client 'difficult'.

However, studies such as that carried out by the OECD (1995) suggest that agencies are, in fact, able to identify those at risk of falling 'through the net' and may be able to estimate numbers. However, the individuals concerned are a disparate group who do not fit agency expectations. They require solutions which take into account the diversity of the whole group and do not compartmentalize problems into, for example, homelessness, offending behaviour or abuse. That does not mean that inter-agency projects for young homeless people or looked after children are wasting their time, but that these projects cannot be fully effective without the support of an inter-agency structure of some kind to sustain clients when they cease to qualify for a particular project's attention.

Thus the group of people defined as 'through the net' tend to move in and out of 'through the netness' over time and according to the problems they experience. Risk factors, as Rutter (1980) pointed out long ago, have a multiplying effect. This was confirmed over a decade later in the OECD's 1995 survey, which gave careful consideration to the question of definitions, since these had to hold across a range of countries and cultures. This survey found substantial agreement about the general nature of what was meant by children and youth 'at risk', defining them as:

> those who are failing at school and who are unsuccessful in making the transition to work and adult life and as a consequence are unlikely to make a full contribution to the active society.

> There are many manifestations of a failure to integrate successfully which include: health problems, substance and drug abuse, crime, early pregnancy and unemployment.
>
> (OECD 1995: 21, 47)

According to this study, the strength of the term lay in its emphasis on the future and on prevention. Recognizing the importance of a developmental perspective, the study suggests that 'that the term "at risk" emphasizes future prospects. It is a predictive concept which assumes the children and pupils "at risk" have certain characteristics which allow them to be identified, but that these characteristics only become a problem when they meet events and conditions that have yet to occur' (OECD 1995: 18). The study only applied the concept of 'at risk' to children and young people whose problems originate in factors in the social environment which, over time, may cumulatively develop into 'within child' variables. In its view, the concept of 'at risk', in emphasizing prevention rather than remedial approaches to the problem, was:

> an optimistic one if it moves the debate forward by recognising the transactional nature of much learning. In the educational context this means that the right educational experiences over time can help to compensate for disadvantage and optimise the chances of success for all pupils.
>
> (p. 19)

On the basis of these definitions, the survey showed, with considerable variation between member countries, figures of between 15 and 30 per cent for children and young people 'at risk'. This tallies with Canadian estimates of 30–40 per cent of 'at risk' young people in urban school populations and 15–20 per cent of rural school students (Mawhinney 1994). According to Mawhinney, there is growing agreement that the factors putting children at risk tend to be interactive and cumulative, culminating most seriously in the transition between adolescence and adulthood. Failure to coordinate agency responses to this is seen as a further factor contributing to the risk.

Thus the search for definitions and an accurate language with which to discuss the needs of vulnerable and neglected children and young people is complex. Here, it is important to the extent that it enables agencies to distinguish between young people 'at risk', a large population, and those among them, a smaller number, at risk of falling 'through the net'. Among the latter, while some succeed, for a small proportion life is never other than hard and distressing, yet their claim on resources is rarely prioritized.

It seems, then, that the question of why or how or to categorize children and young people, and for what purpose, has been sharply debated in the past thirty years. The best known debates have centred on definitions of ethnic minority status, disability, special educational needs and social class. In the context of this study the matter is important, since not all agency services provide universal services for children. Even those that do are obliged to target services and must make difficult choices in an attempt to maintain a balance between upstream and downstream work.

This has been highlighted by, for example, the development of children's services' plans. Moss and Petrie (1997: 4) challenge the 'dominant discourse' concerning children, parents and society. In this discourse, they suggest, children are the private responsibility and the passive dependants of their parents. They are recipients of services.

> These core ideas give a predominant position to two relationships:
> • the relationship between the *child* and her *parents* within the nuclear family; and
> • the relationship between *parent* and the *market*.

Accordingly, they argue, no active place is left for children in services or society.

Moss and Petrie see this reflected in the 1989 Children Act, in which 'parental responsibility is a legally recognized concept . . . but *societal* responsibility is less clearly defined' (Moss and Petrie 1997: 4). They see societal interventions as increasingly piecemeal and targeted, as the role of the state diminishes, placing increased responsibility on individuals to provide for themselves. Therefore, 'children are increasingly exposed to the full forces of the market, with its attendant, inherent and increasing inequalities and insecurities' (p. 5). In this scenario, children are dependent and privatized unless their needs are considered to be 'at risk', 'in need' or requiring 'protection', in which case they become the responsibility of the public. They will then be even more easily construed as weak, poor and helpless.

Moss and Petrie advocate a discourse based on a relationship among children, parents and society in which concepts of the child and of childhood are radically reconstructed. They see the child as a complex human being and a citizen, full of potential and power and of equal value to an adult. The child has rights and, as an active member of a community and society, takes increasing responsibility as an individual and as a family member. Children are valued for who they are and what they will become. Childhood is regarded as an important stage of life in its own right, and children are seen as a social group whose rights need protection and promotion. Parenthood is seen as socially important and parents recognize the public and private function of the role. Civic society values social cohesion, inclusion, reciprocity and democratic participation.

Sleeter argues similarly, in a North American context, for a deconstruction of the 'at risk' label. This is seen as the means whereby the 'dominant discourse' frames 'such children and their families as lacking the cultural and moral resources for success in a presumed fair and open society and as in need of compensatory help from the dominant society' (in Swadener and Lubeck 1995: Foreword). Swadener and Lubeck find that discussions of risk factors and poverty tend not to include 'an interrogation of privilege and the possibility that a more equitable distribution of materials, resources, education, power and self sufficiency may put the stark discrepancies of privilege at risk' (p. 2). Thus for them the term 'at risk' is problematic, and should be replaced with the 'vision of children and families "at promise"' (p. 11).

These concepts require a new approach to services for children, one in which, it can be argued, to target any group independently of others is to undermine the whole framework. Thus terms such as 'at risk', 'in difficulty' or 'in need' reinforce and further entrench the 'dominant discourse'. Hodgkin and Newell (1996), in their report already quoted, recognize that in ratifying the UN Convention on the Rights of the Child in 1991, the United Kingdom government 'recognised the need for co-ordination in the planning of local children's services and has made the process mandatory (although as yet only required for targeted groups of children rather than for all children . . .)' (p. 5). These researchers appear to accept the new discourse as an aim and the need for profound changes in the way in which children's services are structured in this country. They recommend that government strategy for UK children should be founded on the UN convention. In addition to the creation of special structures already discussed, they seek to increase the visibility of children in government, give them political priority and increase the active participation of children in society. In this context, the challenge that children and young people who 'escape from' or 'fall through the net' of agency 'containers' present to policy-makers, managers and practitioners may well become valued for what it is, a unique opportunity to re-examine values, attitudes and practice in relation to children and to concepts of community.

Conclusion

The development of inter-agency cooperation in relation to children and young people suggests some broad generalizations. Where government and

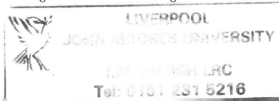

agency policy has tended to reinforce existing structures and the continued fragmentation of services, professional practice, while emphasizing the need for specialist expertise, also acknowledges the need for the development of inter-professionalism and inter-personal skills. Meanwhile, the perspective of young people suggests the need for coordinated services, ecological approaches, increased participation and improved access to professional expertise and advocacy.

Examples of inter-agency practice have, until relatively recently, tended to be small-scale responses to local conditions. Attempts to generalize, or to find links between the scattered, diverse projects of the early 1990s (which continue to be a feature of inter-agency practice) and the current development of large-scale government-led inter-agency strategies are still at an early stage. What lessons have been learnt, and how is past experience being used both to inform and to evaluate current inter-agency practice? Part 2 looks at the detail of what happens at agency boundaries in an attempt to answer these questions.

Note

1 This metaphor comes from the story of the women in a village whose menfolk have been taken away. After many weeks with no news they begin to find bodies floating downstream. Some they save, others are already dead. Eventually a group of them decide to go upstream . . . This story is variously told to suit local situations, but see the play *Widows* by the Argentinian writer Ariel Dorfman (1997).

PART TWO

Making process visible

CHAPTER FOUR

Inter-agency work in practice

Learning from experience

The following account describes an inter-agency project designed to find out what happens on the ground when practitioners try to promote inter-agency cooperation to prevent young people falling 'through the net'. This project had its origins in an initiative set up in the 1980s under the auspices of an Oxford-based charity for ex-prisoners, the Elmore Committee. A group of practitioners had formed a working party to examine the problems they were experiencing in relation to 'difficult to place' (DTP) mentally disturbed adult petty offenders (Vagg 1987). They attributed most of these problems to the failure of agencies to cooperate. They were already well known to each other as members of 'The Network', a meeting held regularly for the large number of people across a range of statutory and non-statutory agencies whose work brought them in contact with DTP people. For Elmore's working party, agency difficulties stemmed from obstacles, legal and otherwise, standing in the way of inter-agency cooperation, even though the avenues for this seemed to exist. The group members, as key agency witnesses, interviewed members of the voluntary sector and other agencies involved with DTP adults to seek their views.

After two years' study, in meetings held once a month, the group recommended the formation of a multidisciplinary panel to 'take continuing responsibility for DTP people referred to it', supported by specialist accommodation (Vagg 1987: 4). On the basis of these proposals and with funding from joint finance, part of the local joint consultative committee structure (discussed on p. 17), a researcher was employed to carry out a feasibility study. However, it soon became apparent that 'if such a [multi-disciplinary] panel could be set up easily, there would have been no need for the project' (Vagg 1987: 5). Accordingly, the nature of the research began to change. What had begun as a proposal for specialist accommodation and some form of multidisciplinary advisory panel became, instead, a detailed study of inter-agency referral processes and an analysis of the obstacles standing in the way of inter-agency cooperation. Identification, assessment and referral, and a continuation of the data collection begun in the preparatory stage all became a vehicle for the discussion of process, of definitions and of agency priorities over resources. Meanwhile, working party members kept their own agencies informed of the project's progress and promoted discussion there of its aims.

In fact, towards the end of the project and continuing after the formal research had ceased, evidence was accumulating which suggested that the problem was not lack of resources, or indeed of inter- or multi-agency meeting points. Agency support for the DTP was increasing, but the coordination required to ensure the effective use of existing resources and to support those who worked with the DTP, in whatever agency context, was missing. What was needed was not a tangible resource such as a building, but the less tangible concept of a coordinating team. Contrary to what had been assumed, resources were adequate but the system was not. It is not easy, however, to attract financial support for systemic solutions, so it was with some relief that, thanks to a windfall unexpectedly landing in the lap of the then DHSS, external funding was eventually secured. This was used to set up a small inter-agency team, the Elmore Community Support Team (ECST), as a two-year pilot, after which local agencies took over its financial support. Fifteen years later, the ECST remains the key player in the coordination of resources for this very vulnerable group of people, a monument to what can be achieved by a determined group of practitioners.

The Elmore experiment was interesting for two reasons. First, the approach used to promote inter-agency cooperation in relation to one client group could, in principle, be applied to another group with equal success. Second, the experience gained from setting up a second project using the same method and based on the same model might suggest solutions to the problems faced by practitioners in their efforts to work across agency boundaries. Mainstream special educational needs coordinators, for example, among many other groups of intra- and inter-agency professionals, are faced every day with the threat of children falling 'through the net'. Could the same approach be replicated with young people? Could a pilot project make process visible in this way and, if so, how and why? Even if the research showed that there was no single systemic solution to the problem of 'through the netness', it seemed that the study of process would contribute to a deeper understanding of what happens at agency boundaries and ultimately, perhaps, to more effective inter-agency practice.

Thus the project sought to examine agency system and process in such a way as to encourage practitioners and policy-makers across agency boundaries to identify problems common to them all and to develop and agree solutions collectively. In other words, the object of the study was to get people involved in inter-agency activity and then to observe their behaviours as they probed agency boundaries. Faced with the acute problems for young people caused by the failure of agencies to cooperate, practitioners often gave the impression of being prevented at a personal level from responding creatively and flexibly to the needs of their clients. They focused on problems rather than solutions. Elmore's methodology had successfully engaged those who thought in terms of problems (and were constrained by a variety of fears and inhibitions) in activities encouraging more flexible behaviours and more productive outcomes.

In the new project for TTN children and young people (referred to here as Elmore II) the intention was to adopt Elmore methodology using a research officer and key witnesses backed by an inter-agency steering group. However, the Elmore emphasis on *process* had also uncovered the outlines of an effective inter-agency *structure*, composed, at that time, of two elements, a coordinating team and an inter-agency network. Superficially at least, the resemblance to the intra-agency coordinating structure already operating within education to meet the needs of children with special educational needs was close enough to warrant further exploration (see Chapter 7). If this was the case, it suggested that Elmore's combination of structure and process could be replicated and that a useful model might emerge which could then be used, for purposes of comparison, with other projects and for evaluation.

Networks and network-broking

Two key Elmore concepts are introduced here, since, taken together, they formed part of the rationale for the model of structured coordination Elmore II had in mind. The first of these, 'The Network', was set up in the early 1980s at a time when the word 'network' was used rather less freely than it is now. It had been created for:

> agencies who recognise that they cannot on their own hope to make significant progress with their most difficult clients e.g. offenders who are homeless, street drinkers, young people adrift from home, and that formal networking is required to meet their needs. The network is a loose structure including a very wide range of agencies working with single people in Oxford. It includes not only housing agencies but day facilities and specialist support and advice services. The 'network' meet through a monthly meeting which is essentially different from an inter-agency meeting in that the network has no power in and of itself, but it can have enormous influence. Many agencies in the 'network' are involved with other parts of the system, but the 'network' itself has no formal links with any other body.
>
> (Derived from Pat Goodwin, co-ordinator of
> the Network, in OCVA 1991: 2)

The Network functioned as a forum for local practitioners where they could raise issues and seek support for matters arising from their practice. With the establishment of an inter-agency team, practitioners had the beginnings of a structure enabling them to coordinate activity, at two levels, on behalf of individuals needing the support of more than one agency. One of the functions of the ECST was *network-broking*, then a highly innovative process. The purpose was to:

- provide a package of care without alienating the agencies,
- ask agencies to take on only what is within their mandate,
- case manage those whose problems are beyond the mandate of a number of agencies.

The ECST accepted that agencies needed the reassurance of knowing that they would only have to do what they had a mandate to do. Whatever was beyond this, the support team would pick up. Much time was spent by the team on self-scrutiny because of the seriousness of the issues raised by the team's work in, for example, the field of civil liberties. When was it right to intervene in the life of a severely disturbed adult? This issue would also arise with teenagers.

DTP clients, it was generally agreed, are likely to be those for whom agencies, at a traditional case meeting, say they can do nothing. Thus it was important for the ECST never to shut a case, open violence apart. Keeping the case open kept the relationship going, however little might be achieved. ECST members were all, apart from the coordinator, seconded from their agencies and, although deroled from whatever agency they came from, were not deskilled. This gave the team independence and added to its credibility. The team did not 'own' anything, but its members, in their role as network brokers, could find out from each agency what provision was available and could then pursue this vigorously on behalf of the client.

Thus Elmore I had provided some evidence suggesting that solutions to the problem of those who 'fall through the net' depend on effective systems as well as on effective people and processes. A source of independent funding had also been significant: at a time of growing financial constraint, an innovative proposal could be presented to the agencies as an attractive 'no cost' pilot project. This achievement owed everything to the collective courage and flair of the working party. Its members were creative thinkers and confident professionals drawn together by their shared frustration at the inability of agencies to cooperate and the seeming lack of agency commitment to clients they cared about. This united them in a common determination to arrive at a solution. They did not feel bound by either bureaucracy or personal inhibitions and encouraged each other to think critically, objectively and constructively about what their client group required of the agencies and how agencies could be persuaded to reinterpret their role in relation to this group. They relied on the success of their practical experiment to change agency and practitioner attitude and behaviour – an early example, in Huxham's (1996) phrase, of 'collaborative advantage'. Without the structural element of the team and its longstanding network, its network broking capacities would, however, have been severely limited.

Replicating the model for children and young people 'through the net': Elmore II

Inspired by this example, a group of practitioners, equally frustrated by problems of inter-agency cooperation in relation to 'through the net' children and young people, set out to replicate the model. Making the case for it was relatively straightforward. The Elton Report into Discipline in Schools (1989) acted as a catalyst, by raising awareness locally of the problems caused by the failure of agencies to cooperate. Although Elton was primarily directed at the education service, concern about inter-agency cooperation in relation to truancy, discipline and disaffection, though difficult to enumerate in those pre-league table days, was general among all the agencies in the run-up to the implementation of the 1989 Children Act. Other factors, such as recession and increased child poverty and family stress, heightened awareness of the extent of children's needs and led to calls for greater agency accountability. In this climate, the heads of the relevant agencies (health, education and social services) agreed to the formation of a group of middle managers to study the issue of inter-agency cooperation. With hindsight, it is possible that senior managers had not fully considered the implications of this decision, or, indeed, of how little contact there was at that time between agencies within even one small city. This seemed paradoxical given the amount of inter-agency activity practitioners had, according to their own description, been involved in. Thus one of the frustrations for Elmore II was that Elmore I was so little known or understood by those working with young people below the age of 17, even though one agency, social services, was common to both groups, and there was some overlap (e.g. detached youth workers) between client groups.

In assessing the current state of inter-agency activity and attitudes locally, the Elmore 'ground rules' were adopted:

- to use the steering group as an example of good inter-agency practice, with each member making a commitment to think 'inter-agency' in their daily professional work;
- to promote debate within each agency on the aims and objectives of the project;
- to encourage agency ownership of the project so that each agency, particularly the key areas of health, education and social services, could invest fully in the project and its development.

This collaborative and participatory approach enabled steering group members to act as both role models for cooperation and key informants for the research. As the project progressed and cooperation became more challenging, this role became more difficult to sustain, reinforcing the importance, in the early stages, of the habit-forming commitment to 'think inter-agency'.

Involving others: local views on inter-agency cooperation

At this stage the problem appeared to centre on:

- the difficulties individual agencies experience in helping young people and their families whom they may feel are on the margins of their responsibility;
- the lack of support, in terms of time and resources, for inter-agency cooperation to take place in all cases which call for it (OCVA 1991: 2).

As with Elmore I, a series of interviews with practitioners were used to:

- assess the commitment of each agency to working collaboratively and investigate whatever obstacles stand in the way of inter-agency cooperation;
- assess the needs of those identified as falling between the agency nets in order to expose gaps in existing services;
- suggest other resources or initiatives not at present provided or not part of current practice;
- assess the demand likely to be made on resources over a specified period of time (e.g. five years) (p. 4).

Representatives of agencies such as youth work, social services, education social work and the health service and leaders of other local inter-agency initiatives were invited to steering group meetings for detailed discussions. Their responses included much that was familiar as well as new insights, gradually building a picture from practitioner experience of the then state of inter-agency cooperation.

These responses revealed a complex web of formal and informal inter- and intra-agency meetings. Between education, health and social services, eight regular meetings attended by more than two agencies were recorded, with further 'pairings' between, for example, social workers and education social workers. Each agency was also connected with a further inter-agency meeting reaching a different arena, not necessarily connected with the other two. For example, social workers attended the young homelessness forum and detached youth workers attended the network for 'difficult to place' adults, each extensive networks in themselves. Meetings took place at policy and practitioner level and each agency had its own internal web of meetings and team meetings. Sometimes these developed specific purposes; for example, at team meetings in-service training was an important activity. The main foci for inter-agency activity seemed to be school liaison and child protection with a specialist network for young homelessness.

Those interviewed considered that inter-agency networking was welcomed and needed, but that it was difficult and time consuming in practice. Large meetings were considered unwieldy. Obstacles to inter-agency cooperation centred on professionalism, time, confidentiality and ambiguities in relation to the definition of 'children'. These interviews took place during the run-up to the implementation of the 1989 Children Act in 1991. This had engendered a flurry of inter-agency training and the discovery that 'each agency is tackling the Children Act differently'. Confusion over professional and agency boundaries was mentioned frequently, with parochialism, lack of confidence and confusion about roles and responsibilities featuring as the main criticisms. Interviewees complained of the difficulty different professions have of defining what they do.

> People do not want to be rigid, but cannot do everything and need to accept their and other's limitations. Having accepted a clear set of principles about this there is then the need for anxiety management and to avoid blaming oneself and others.
>
> (OCVA 1991: 10)

Each agency, they reported, tends to perceive different problems with the same child, resulting in referrals to different agencies. In some cases there were difficulties 'over what each agency expects from each other and about what should be done about the disparities and overlaps. This can produce real inequities of care' (p. 12). Being prepared to work together, while at the same time keeping 'clear what their real professional boundaries are', was regarded as important. Problems were also caused in situations where one agency initiates and another has to carry out practice; for example, in relation to school refusal or emotional and behavioural difficulties.

When interviewees were asked how cooperation might be improved, the suggestions were typical of those in similar studies of the time: improved systems for managing inter-professional boundaries, time and confidentiality. A forum where issues such as differences of philosophy between agencies could be discussed and practical ways forward could be considered was proposed to increase understanding of what constitutes good inter-agency action.

> good inter-agency work was more likely to be found where different agencies felt able to nail their colours to the mast and be clear about what their function was. There was also a role for managers in setting formal inter-agency groups which could frame and discuss general problems leaving the sorting out of individual cases to the informal 'worker to worker' level. It is at this informal level that detailed, often highly confidential work can take place and at which plans can be put forward which can then inform discussion as to what future action might be taken at a more formal level.
>
> (OCVA 1991: 15)

Finally, in relation to teenagers, the view was that a more creative and flexible resource was needed, with more hostels and workers. Young people themselves needed confidence building and assertiveness training to help them make better use of the information and resources available.

Insights gained were sometimes unexpected, emphasizing the need for deeper probing along agency boundaries than could be achieved by an interview.

Sometimes a finding at first neglected emerged later in a different context. The following example will be of interest to special educational needs teachers, since it draws attention to an inadequacy in the system for managing statements of special educational need. A 'joint practice group' consisting of representatives from education, health and social services explored inter-agency working through a study of the 20 most difficult young people in the county, as perceived by each agency. This group found that an unsatisfactory outcome for a young person is frequently arrived at when agencies meet and reach a decision which is a compromise. The compromise was more likely to meet the *agencies'* need for a decision than the *child's* needs. This drew attention to the distinction between a *case meeting* convened so that all the agencies involved can be present, for discussion, and a referral to a *case manager* who will, on behalf of the agencies as a result of discussion, search out the best course of action for the child. This example showed how a case manager could act as advocate, and broker, negotiating the package of support required to guide the young person back into the network of provision. However, even if the term network-broking had been used, there was, at the time, no structure within which such a role could be played. This void in the organization of services endorsed the appropriateness of the concept of a support team as an essential element in an enabling coordinating structure.

At the end of its first stage, Elmore II noted that:

- in spite of a plethora of inter-agency groups dealing with children and young people in difficulty, there is no one agency, service or team responsible for the care of these very vulnerable young people, who could support those who slip through existing provision and guide them back into it;
- most inter-agency work that is happening is less effective than it might be due to lack of structured co-ordination, to the extent that workers can be said to be suffering from 'meeting fatigue'.

(OCVA 1991)

In response, the project recommended, and proposed to investigate:

- the setting up of a multi-disciplinary network for the age group 12–18 years, on the lines of the network already in existence for those over the age of 17;
- the setting up of a community support team to whom referral could be made of the cases who most severely tax the agencies endeavouring to help them, and whose staff would guarantee to act as case managers on behalf of these young people, undertaking the case work required to meet their needs and generate a network of support;
- the further development of training opportunities for those working across professional boundaries.

(OCVA 1991: Summary)

These recommendations were complex, interconnected and demanding to put into operation. By encouraging the heads of service to act on them through continued support of the project, Elmore II was embarking on a risky venture. Principally, there was the danger that senior managers, or others not connected, or not in sympathy, with the project would focus on the elements which were easiest, or least expensive, to implement. Seeing the importance of the package as a whole was difficult, making independent sources of support and advice especially important.

The question of numerical data was at that time highly contentious. This created a problem, since uncertainty about the number of TTN young people made it difficult to make the case on behalf of a group it was all too frequently in the agencies' interest to ignore. It was not ignored, however, by the city secondary headteachers. Motivated by city-wide problems of school attendance and the transfer of pupils between schools they set up their own multi-agency group, for which they too required figures. As a result they agreed, in advance of the 1993 Education Act's requirement to do so, to share, at least within the privacy of their meetings, statistical information on attendance and exclusion. Thus it was possible for Elmore II to estimate that were a youth support team, modelled on the ECST, to be set up in the city, it would have about 50 young people of compulsory school age on its books at any one time, from a larger pool of about 150 young people at risk of falling 'through the net'. Out of a population of approximately 150,000 this was a tiny proportion, insignificant except in terms of the severity of each individual case and the cost to society of doing nothing. It was recognized that this number was a minimum, however, since problems (noted by other local projects such as 'Girls in Difficulty', an inter-agency group addressing the problems of girls out of school) for young people post-16 were known to be severe and increasing.

Work with young people and agencies

With financial support from the Joseph Rowntree Foundation, to employ a research officer, the real venture to the boundaries dividing agency from agency began. For its second, development stage, the project brief was to:

1 Set up an inter-agency network.
2 Identify gaps in services.
3 Suggest other resources and initiatives not yet provided or not part of current practice.

As an indication of the extent of inter-agency activity taking place at the time, the research officer, in the first three months alone, had contacted 36 different agency groups or individuals, and had attended 16 different inter-agency forums concerned with children and young people.

Young people under 16

In order to explore young people's perspective on agency cooperation, 28 young people and their parent/guardians were contacted by letter, of whom eight could not be interviewed for various reasons. Of the 20 interviewed, five could not be followed up because of the risk of undermining agency work currently taking place. For the remaining 15 permission was sought from the family and young person.

> He was offending while truanting from school. A mixture of the two. In the end we felt like tennis balls because Education said it was a social problem and Social Services said it was an education problem, and we were just going backwards and forwards from one to another.
>
> (Roaf and Lloyd 1995)

The case studies (see also Chapter 6), in which participants made vivid use of metaphor to illustrate their experiences, convinced senior managers, heads of service and local government politicians, as perhaps nothing else could have done, that the failure of agencies to cooperate presented real problems, affecting real people. These problems were summarized as follows:

- Young people with multiple needs require the services of more than one agency.
- Young people are defined by individual agency boundaries rather than by an analysis of their need, and therefore tend to be seen as on the margin, or outside of, any one particular service provision.
- Young people and their families are not aware of their rights and responsibilities.
- There are sometimes lengthy delays in assessing the needs of a young person.
- Young people get 'lost' in the system.
- The needs of ethnic minority young people are not prioritized by any one agency. In instances where they need specialist support they find themselves outside mainstream agency provision.
- Young people suffering from mental health problems are particularly vulnerable.
- Young people experience delays in assessment or provision through the assessment process leading to a Statement under the 1981 Education Act (Lloyd 1994: 35–7).

In the research officer's view these issues were not new: 'they have all been previously identified by workers in the field and by the families and young people involved' (p. 40).

Young people over 16

Little was known about the number of young people 'through the net' post-16, even though a number of projects were involved with them. However, evidence from Elmore I and its Network for DTP adults estimated that, at any one time, there were approximately 150 DTP adults in Oxford (Vagg 1987). Elmore II was interested in the earlier experiences of older teenagers, particularly their experience of statutory services, and hoped that work with this age group would shed light on agency activity with the younger age groups. These were young people caught sight of by agencies only fleetingly, or who got lost in the system. The research officer notes:

> Initially, I felt that much of my research with young people over 16 would be among those who were known to at least one of the main agencies e.g. SSD or the ESW service, and therefore could not be seen to have truly 'fallen through the net' of provision in a literal sense. In fact these studies revealed that many young people are left with no appropriate support except basic provision.
>
> (Lloyd 1993: 66)

The study involved about 30 young people over a six-month period. The techniques used were participatory, to build up trust through group work and to encourage frank and honest discussion. The study introduced Elmore II to a further range of agencies and networks involved with young people, including the police, probation, housing and voluntary sector provision such as the Night Shelter. It also became the project's point of entry into border country between the 'Network' for adults and the one proposed for adolescents. It established that: 'for many young people, at a crucial age of development, especially as far as education and housing is concerned, delays in intervention, lack of resources and lack of co-ordination, means that for a significant time these young people . . . in effect fall through the net' (p. 75).

The young people were clear that they wanted educational opportunities, especially the skills needed to cope with a college environment, help in combining child care with education and/or work and a range of facilities such as counselling, drop-in facilities, housing and welfare benefits, independent housing, family planning and parenting skills. Most had no direct access to any provision and had no key worker to help them with support, information and advice, a function we see developing today through Connexions (DfES 2001a). Although facilities were being developed in the area, it seemed that this age group was even more in need of inter-agency support than those of school age, and that an adolescent network and youth support team which would bridge the pre- and post-16 gap could be a key ingredient in any preventative inter-agency strategy.

Thus issues arising from the work with young people centred on their need for a holistic service, to be aware of their rights, to experience the assertion of these rights in the communities in which they lived, to be consulted and to have their wishes and feelings taken into account. Young people looked, in short, for commitment, advocacy and respect from the professionals and agencies with whom they had contact. The simplicity of their needs thus contrasts starkly with the complexity of the concerns of the professionals.

Working with the agencies

Although the agencies and organizations contacted accepted the concept of inter-agency work and most worked at various levels to develop this, there was concern about difficulties in agreeing a definitive description of the client group they catered for. This made referrals a frustrating exercise: (a) for the other agencies, which are unclear of the specific role of each agency; and (b) for the referral agency that receives an inappropriate referral. The agencies were also confused about theoretical and practical responsibility, individual work methods, day-to-day pressures of work and overlapping administrative boundaries. Even within a single local authority, intra- and inter-agency groups appeared to be uncoordinated and to work independently of each other, leading to calls for open information sharing and better communication. A lack of understanding of different agency priorities, the inability to share information freely and a lack of understanding of professional status and the role of different agencies were specific issues mentioned.

Interviews with practitioners from a range of agencies made sense of the problems revealed in the case studies. From them a list, corresponding to the list of problems faced by the young people, was drawn up:

- Practitioners are unsure which specialist agency to refer to.
- Individual disciplines within an agency have problems defining what they offer in relation to each other.
- Responsibility for service delivery is vertically managed, causing difficulty for collaboration across agencies.
- Agencies are not always clear about the limits of their responsibility and therefore tend to spend too much time working on their own with young people with multiple needs, and too little time in cooperation with other agencies to make effective joint plans in the cases which call for this.
- Each agency has statutory responsibilities. This can create difficulties in co-ordinating provision and developing a holistic care plan for a young person.
- Each agency has its own culture, language, aims and objectives and priorities.
- Each individual worker has different pressures and incentives placed on them.
- Agencies find it difficult to accept responsibility for seeing a 'case' through the 'system'.
- Different agencies use different screening methods to control their intake of clients. This gatekeeping of provision gives some agencies access to provision and others none.
- There is a lack of coordination between school transfers and a lack of continuity of approach with reference to school exclusions.
- Agencies often find it difficult to agree 'ownership' of the 'case'.
- There is no one agency, team or service responsible for the care of these vulnerable young people, which can support those who slip through existing provision and guide them back into it.
- Different agencies share different responsibilities for young people at 16.
- There is limited understanding of what inter-agency work means in terms of skills and practice and of its potential to alleviate problems of the agencies as distinct from those of the young people.
- There is a lack of strategic planning across agencies.
- Agencies do not hold the same information and have difficulty passing information to one another.
- Conflicting legislation and financial constraints have created additional barriers to multi-agency cooperation.
- Each agency holds its own budget and few mechanisms exist for joint financing.
- Agencies are still uncertain about their roles, particularly in the context of purchasing and providing (Lloyd 1994: 30–5).

The formidable array of problems identified by both the agencies and the young people can, however, be grouped into four sets of generic issues, all of which affect all the parties to inter-agency cooperation. These issues concern:

- legislation;
- strategic and operational matters;
- professional practice;
- financial arrangements.

Agency problems could be further reduced to issues of structure and process. It thus seemed even more important to establish a coordinating framework to help agencies to bring these different aspects of their work into a functional relationship. For the agencies, however, the main subject of this study, Elmore II exposed the problems caused by uncoordinated approaches to cooperation.

> This lack of structured co-ordination creates problems of working collaboratively which is often put down to problems with individuals or a particular agency. A whole agency can be scapegoated for the failure of an inter-agency project to be effective. The hostility and suspicion which then develops further hinders the development of successful inter-agency co-operation and the workers retreat to their own 'patches' where they feel safer and more able.
>
> (Lloyd 1994: 30)

Agency solutions: developing a coordinating structure

Setting up a network

On the strength of this evidence, a local network was set up, organized along the same lines as its role model, Elmore I's 'Network'. It soon established itself as a meeting point, providing opportunities for discussion of current issues and circulating its directory and newsletter to over 70 agencies, projects and individuals involved with young people in difficulty. Because of its open membership, it was able, as anticipated, to facilitate communication and feedback within and among all the agencies, statutory and non-statutory. This feature was particularly valued by voluntary sector workers on short-term contracts, an expanding group in the political and organizational world of the 1990s. Such practitioners need to be reassured that their work will be followed through by others, preferably within the statutory sector, when their own contracts end. 'Purchaser' members of the Network were frequently able to arrange this. Thus a key finding was that: 'When agencies agree to collaborate over individuals with complex difficulties, they bring their collective experience and determination to bear. The creative solutions which arise, generate improvements for everyone' (Roaf and Lloyd 1995).

By providing regular opportunities to discuss issues as they arose, Elmore II's Adolescent Network enabled its members to address them in a practical way. If, as research has long suggested (e.g. Welton 1985), workers who meet regularly have more knowledge of each other's role and more understanding of priorities within different organizations, and are more trusting of colleagues, then this kind of network provides these opportunities. Collectively then, the new network, like its counterpart for DTP adults, formalized informal networks, identified gaps in provision and responded to these through partnership and information sharing.

Youth support team (YST)

The key issue concerned the third task Elmore II had set itself, that the research should 'suggest other resources/initiatives not yet provided'. The project's evaluators noted that the youth support team model had 'drawn some hostility from agencies who feel threatened (one view) or who feel the proposal is unnecessary (another view)' (Armstrong and Moon 1993: 12). The majority view from within Elmore II, and from its advisory group, was that the model of linked team and network was sound and would provide the coordinating structure required. However, there was strong opposition. In the early to mid-1990s, intra-agency teams in all the primary care agencies had good reason to feel threatened by the proposal, since inter-agency activity was an important element in much of their ordinary work anyway, and cuts in public spending were increasingly difficult to manage. For some, evidence of the number of young people 'through the net' was regarded as proof that inter-agency *coordination* was needed, while for others it was seen as proof of the need to improve inter-agency *cooperation* as part of improved *intra*-agency practice.

What those in favour of inter-agency coordinating structures found most difficult to explain to those opposed to them was that no one *inside* any agency, with the possible exception of the detached youth workers, could easily leave their agency duties to follow a young person into the rough ground between agency playing fields. Even if they ventured out, as some did in practice, they could not stay there with the young person for the length of time required to develop the flexible packages of support needed to bring them back into an agency. Anyone who tried this would be regarded as acting in breach of their statutory agency duties, or at the very least acting beyond the call of duty. Yet unless someone undertook the job of network-broking, young people slipped 'through the net' and stayed there.

The majority of agency practitioners venturing into inter-agency territory also found themselves unfamiliar with the legislation, culture, language and resources of the other agencies they then had to do business with. This created its own problems. The knowledge and interpersonal skills required for network-broking among the agencies had to be learnt, and subsequent action required inter-agency authority which didn't exist. What the research exposed was a plethora of inter-agency *meetings* with no inter-agency *structure* to connect them.

Elmore I had successfully provided this missing ingredient and after experience of it agency fears had been allayed. Elmore II had already begun to replicate this model and members of the Adolescent Network, the first building block in this inter-agency 'building', were in favour of its completion, having seen what could be achieved. In principle, it would have been possible, with agency agreement, to form a small specialist inter-agency resource by regrouping representatives from existing intra-agency teams (school special needs teams, educational social workers and youth work teams in education, youth justice and adolescent teams in social services, community health workers). But this proposal meant asking the primary care agencies to share the cost at a very difficult time for them. Local government review was expected to change administrative boundaries and financial constraints were pressing so heavily on agencies that existing teams, especially in education and social services, were hard pressed to maintain core services. In this situation dilemmas about agency purpose were acute. Should some staff and/or resources be transferred to an inter-agency team set up in the interest of the very small, if needy, minority, or should resources remain within the agencies in the interest of the majority? Was it better to retain resources within agencies for preventative work and crisis management there, or could some of this be more effectively managed through inter-agency coordination?

In fact, social services, the agency suffering most severely from cuts in public spending, supported the proposal most enthusiastically. The effect of the spending squeeze, coupled with the implementation of the 1989 Children Act and the need to provide for children at risk of child abuse, had focused attention on those most in need. Social services were thus better able than others to recognize the potential drain on the system caused by young people 'through the net'. For them, any strategy designed to improve inter-agency coordination would help.

Meanwhile, the police and health authorities, both conscious of the huge cost to their services of, for example, a persistent young offender or a teenage pregnancy, were strongly in favour of the proposal. However, this support may have stemmed from a perception of the problem in financial terms as a drain on resources. By contrast, their colleagues in education and social services saw the problem in more personal terms, with young people in need claiming their daily care and attention. Consequently, the health services and police may have felt less involved personally or professionally, were less easily threatened and more inclined to support the idea. In the event, majority opinion, in favour of doing something radical, prevailed. This led Elmore II to explore, with the headteachers' group, the proposal for a youth support team in the modified form of a pilot inter-agency panel.

Inter-agency processes

Given local concerns, the idea of an inter-agency pilot panel for case management and network-broking along the lines of Elmore I was attractive. For the schools, Elmore II's members and research officer brought valuable inter-agency skills and knowledge. In return, the pilot panel provided an opportunity to introduce inter-agency processes and promote the idea of an inter-agency coordinating structure among the city headteachers, an increasingly powerful group since the introduction of local financial management in 1991. They were now the main budget holders, not the LEA. If money was to come from education to fund a youth support team or panel, some would have to come from the city schools. Thus, mindful of the benefits to be gained by positive responses to agency needs, Elmore II agreed to commit time and energy to helping practitioners to set up, manage and evaluate the work of the inter-agency panel, as a six-month pilot.

Panel purpose

The panel operated in many respects much as the original proposal for a team would have done. Elmore II described it as:

> a multi-agency initiative which seeks to support those young people for whom there is a breakdown in education, such as to give school little hope of reintegration, and for whom there are no resources at present or where potential breakdown would cause similar problems.
>
> (Lloyd 1993: 82–3)

Its key features were that:

- membership was multi-agency;
- referrals were made through the schools to a monthly meeting of the panel;
- independent assessors were appointed to gather information about individual cases, and present this to the panel, who then recommended multi-agency packages of support;
- progress reports on the young people were received by the panel at subsequent meetings and further action was planned.

From an inter-agency position, the panel remained, even though multi-agency in its membership, firmly within the territory of education. Therefore, although it succeeded in giving its members experience of inter-agency processes, it did not, and perhaps could not, take its members into inter-agency territory. In this respect, the experiment was, first, not genuinely inter-agency. Second, some of its members may have been, however unintentionally, left with the impression that it was. At the time, discussion of this type would have seemed incomprehensibly esoteric to busy practitioners. Elmore II members were obliged to accept this, and to pursue their own debate on this subject with agency senior managers and heads of service. Third, while the research covered young people aged from 12 to 18, the panel was principally concerned with young people of compulsory school age.

However, there were benefits. Although it appeared expensive and unproductive, with many people involved and only 16 cases referred over the five months of the panel's operation, it was recognized that:

- pilot work is expensive;
- it produces questions to be answered and further work to be done;
- there had been a history of everyone doing their own thing in separate patches – this brought people together and a number of people were able to talk to each other who had not had that opportunity before.

The panel's self-evaluation (Roaf 1999b) proposed that, given the expense, a decision should be made as to whether to revert to the previous situation, or 'acknowledge that there had been improvements. Young people were being pulled back into the system.' Existing structures, with the addition of an inter-agency worker, created the climate in which schools deal with the majority, educational social workers deal with those beginning to slip away and:

we pick up those TTN using panel working methods . . . this enables us to throw the rule book away and get on with it. The sort of inter-agency work the panel was engaged with produced exciting packages and got together people who could say 'this might work', 'this key worker might do it'.

The panel noted that its policy had been to look at whatever cases the schools sent, to look at everything known about the young person and at whatever could be done before making a decision. Dangers to be aware of were, first, that schools might relinquish responsibility for the young people referred to the panel, and, second, that the schools might themselves feel marginalized. Other difficulties noted were the need to involve the health service and the need to affirm the role of the ESW service in establishing who was 'through the net'.

The panel's self-evaluation raised a number of issues. The definition of TTN did not, in the panel's experience, fully describe the students referred. In several cases the panel had:

> kick started services into action but in the majority of cases there was a network of agencies involved already, but these had not been able to offer the appropriate response. In these cases the Panel had a role in establishing a needs assessment and an action plan through the Independent Assessor's report.

Other issues concerned improvements to existing intra-agency methods for early intervention, preventative work and inter-agency problems over confidentiality. The panel's role in relation to young people post-16 raised the kind of questions we are familiar with today in terms of 'triage' (Gillborn and Youdell 2000). Were they to be considered beyond the reach of help (one view), or as an indication of the need for early, pre-school preventative strategies (another view)? A third view recognized that some young people post-16 were already parents, so that the problem was, in effect, indivisible. If post-16 was panel responsibility, then establishing who the appropriate key worker would be was a difficulty. If not, there was a transfer issue. Panel members were encouraged to progress these issues through the Adolescent Network.

Independent assessors and key workers

Elmore II's decision to become involved with the panel was taken because of the opportunity this would provide to explore inter-agency process. The panel did indeed achieve this objective, exposing inter-professional and inter-personal points of contact, as well as misunderstandings and incompatibilities. Many of these centred on values and professional ethics expressed through a range of positive and negative behaviours. However difficult and potentially damaging some of the reactions were at the time, the object of the research was to expose and work with these issues rather than mask them. Issues which triggered the sharpest reactions tended to focus on inter-agency case work and management, confidentiality and the interface between agencies explored by the independent assessors.

The role of the independent assessor (based on the work of the MARS project in Dundee: see Chapter 5) required trial and error in order to tease out its key elements and to ensure that these did not conflict either with agency responsibilities or with inter-agency panel aims to achieve practical action for the young people. The panel appointed independent assessors, allocated cases to them and received their reports. On the basis of the reports the panel then identified key workers. The minutes (Roaf 1999b) record that: 'by having an independent assessor the panel would be able to tap resources hitherto unobtainable e.g. [we] would not previously have thought of using a voluntary youth worker [as a key worker].' The independent assessor, a network broker, was an advocate and enabler who could:

> by pulling things together . . . enable the keyworker to draw on other agencies for support and assistance . . . the key workers knew the contacts and got access to things that weren't usually on the agenda. We went out of our way to use unusual keyworkers who were more sensitive and were at a better starting point.

The use of 'unusual' key workers was an important element in the panel's successes with young people. The panel's job was to identify, from the independent assessor's report and their own experience, who, if anyone, had a positive relationship with the young person 'through the net'. In some cases this person had no statutory responsibilities but could be supported by someone who did. In many instances this was often initially the most effective means of helping a young person back into the support network. The panel's success therefore depended on the permission agency practitioners gave each other to act creatively. There are important parallels and points of contrast here with the developing role of Connexions' personal advisers appointed to work with teenagers (DfES 2001a).

The panel's view was that as its work developed so did the benefits. For example:

> a clearer understanding of the systems which already existed in different agencies was developed and, in part, usefully co-ordinated for particular referrals . . . Extensive ad hoc discussion took place during the life of the panel . . . By accessing the work of other agencies the range of programmes was improved and better. Panel members characterised the initiative as providing 'spin offs/creative thinking . . . it developed its own momentum/dynamic so after a while the panel was thinking more creatively'.

Phrases such as 'got more information', 'got more creative' and 'widened terms of referral' were used to describe successes during the course of the pilot. Less successful aspects related to the time scale of the project. Thus it was not always clear if successful intervention would result in long-term change for the young person; nor, significantly, had there been 'any general system improvement'. Other issues mentioned were that referrals were geared to education and not to difficulties outside school. This could lead to a gap in provision. Some schools had not referred, considering they were able to contain students in school even though help was needed for the home situation. Transfer arrangements between schools still needed attention, as did confidentiality between agencies. This problem had been circumvented for the panel by all members, if not already local authority employees, being formally attached to a relevant agency. Improved practice was noted in the area of special educational needs and more reliable access to the curriculum for late entrants, poor attenders and young people with emotional and behavioural difficulties.

Developing a model for sustainable inter-agency coordination

The six-month pilot had functioned, as anticipated, as an embryonic youth support team. Demands on time and the skills required for assessment, and for the support of key workers, had been greater than expected, however. The intention had been for a number of independent assessors to be involved. In fact, because these proved difficult to find and required a high level of inter-agency professional skill, the research officer did most of the assessment.

However, panel participants had gained confidence in inter-agency work and were keen to incorporate their new skills into their own work within agencies. Much depended on the emotional and financial climate within agencies. Those who recognized that they could not do everything on their own tended not to feel professionally threatened by the existence of young people TTN and were keen to move forward to a YST despite the need to contribute personnel and/or cash to it. These agencies also recognized that the YST could attract funding from agencies that might not normally have contributed directly to the welfare of young people. Agencies which Elmore II had failed to persuade or reassure retreated behind agency boundaries. Without additional money, they were not prepared to support the transfer of agency resources to an inter-agency group.

This proved to be a major problem for education and can be attributed to the introduction of local financial management in schools. Before 1991, schools were centrally financed by LEAs, which could use budget surpluses to support a number of initiatives promoting action research, curriculum development or equal opportunities. Indeed, Oxfordshire had a history of successful projects of this kind (Leeson 1989). After devolution to individual school budgets this became more difficult, as schools became relatively more powerful and less inclined to cooperate with each other. Young people TTN were not a high priority for most schools and the 50 or so present at any one time in the area tended to be concentrated in only a few, already hard-pressed and hard-up, schools. Education's existing intra-agency workers were starved of cash for the same reasons and concerns were beginning to emerge about possible effects on exam results of disaffection and truancy. Thus the headteachers' acceptance of Elmore II's help in carrying out the pilot was a disconcerting mixture of concern for young people in difficulty and fear of what that commitment might involve in terms of resources. In the event, with funding for the research project about to end, and with further cuts expected to agency and school budgets, caution prevailed.

Elmore II, and the inter-agency panel it facilitated, had, none the less, raised the profile of children and young people in difficulty locally. Practitioners had gained experience of inter-agency process and had improved intra-agency practice. In their evaluation, after its first year, Armstrong and Moon (1993) record the project's 'significant influence in raising awareness of the importance of inter-agency co-operation'. The project was seen to be dealing with vexed issues, 'functioning as an important legitimator of activity . . . Without exception, all the agencies saw benefits accruing from their involvement with the project.' This had 'directly and indirectly resulted in changed policy/practices to promote co-operation'. Practitioners noted, for example, that the project 'hasn't got the power to enforce but it has the power to influence by persuasion . . . The project has done something desperately needed and out of it something positive will come. [It has] identified gaps in the existing system and brought people together in one forum.' One agency identified the project as: 'a highly significant factor in promoting the development of a real youth strategy in the area'.

Nonetheless, despite this positive evaluation, one very significant area of difficulty remained. Senior managers could each, it transpired, support the project on behalf of all, or parts of, their own agency, but could not easily achieve this jointly. What was missing, as will be obvious to today's reader, was the policy-making element. Whether an inter-agency policy-making body would have supported the development of a YST at that time is open to question, but the potential significance of such a group as a key element in any inter-agency coordinating structure was becoming clear.

From that point on, Elmore II's survival became less important than finding out more about how such models worked and whether they could be replicated elsewhere. Much had been learnt about how a coordinating structure can integrate upstream and downstream work (see page 56), how the crucial communication links between inter-agency policy-making, case work management and networking can be created and maintained, and how the roles of coordinator, network broker, independent assessor and key worker can be played out for the benefit of children and young people in the frequently dangerous rough ground between agency boundaries. As a model, it had already proved its use as a training tool. Practitioners readily identified themselves in a system in which policy-making, case work and networking were key elements. They could identify, in the roles they each played in their own work, the roles of independent assessors, key workers and network brokers, and they could see how the formalization of previously informal networks could help them as practitioners, and in terms of professional development. Finally, they could see how the interplay of upstream and downstream work affected all their decision-making.

Elmore II had arrived at a different destination from the one intended, but it had raised the stakes and achieved considerable influence and credibility, and was able to disband knowing that fresh life could be given to its objectives through dissemination and training. These ideas have since reappeared in new settings and different forms in, for example, the intra-agency initiatives of the local EAZ (Glenny 2001) and in the success of a rural Elmore III (see Chapter 6). The elusive goal of collaborative advantage, could, it seemed, be achieved.

CHAPTER FIVE

Inter-agency projects: characteristics of good practice

Inter-agency projects for children and young people 'at risk'

Throughout the life of Elmore II, its steering group looked for similar projects to identify characteristics of good practice and organizational structure. However, in the late 1980s, as Gill and Pickles (1989) noted in their study of Scottish youth strategy, then at the cutting edge of inter-agency collaborative activity, 'collaborative practice with young people in trouble is much advocated yet rarely practised' (Introduction). Thus, although the practice of inter-agency working was gathering momentum, encouraged by pressure group activity and the implementation of the 1989 Children Act, the political climate of the time meant that comparable projects were few and far between.

Inter-agency activity, as we have seen, has, until recently, tended to focus on categories such as young offenders, homelessness, looked after or truants. A publication listing community programmes for young people and juvenile offenders records over 200 programmes, of which only a few are concerned with young people 'at risk' (Martin 1997). Even now the focus tends to be on local needs of specific groups identified by agencies, and attention is less commonly directed towards children as a whole. In an NFER audit of a wide range of local inter-agency activity, Atkinson et al. (2001) identify 11 types, of which only three do not specify a target group, addressing instead universal provision, such as health or access to counselling advice and mentoring. For the purpose of this study, projects contemporaneous with Elmore II and resembling it in clientele were selected for comparison. These are presented in Table 5.1 and are briefly described here.

Table 5.1 Inter-agency projects: comparison

Project	MARS	Surrey Youth Link	Mid Glamorgan	Exeter Youth Support Team
Background	Established (Dundee) 1983; central government funding, later local agencies and Barnardo's.	Established 1986; central government funding. Surrey County Council after 1992.	Established 1989.	Established 1979; an Urban Aid Grant.
Aim	Offer alternatives to young people in danger of being removed from their communities.	Promote greater social awareness amongst disaffected or difficult pupils; an inter-disciplinary approach aims to avoid labelling young people. Maintain young people within school. Strengthen existing links between schools and other agencies or create these.	Address problems of crime, alcohol and substance abuse re health and lifestyles of young people. Gain insights into young people's views on these issues. Exploratory and descriptive investigation to raise questions about service delivery and practice.	Divert juvenile offenders from the Criminal Justice System and the courts.
Clientele	High-risk children and their families, e.g. adolescent boys out of school/rejected by residential establishments, children under ten with school difficulties/'poorly parented', children and young people sexually abused.	'Disaffected', 'difficult' or 'disruptive' young people.	Secondary school students.	Potential and actual juvenile offenders, recognizes that the majority of young people who come to the attention of the team will, in time, become responsible members of society.
Inter-agency organization	Explicitly inter-agency team. Five practitioners from a range of agencies. Supported by a management group funded by local agencies and Barnardo's. Procedural and policy framework for collaboration to support practitioners and ensure improvements are implemented.	Multidisciplinary team based in Education. Complex inter-agency management, referral and meetings structure.	Three multi-agency committees and a multi-agency Survey Steering Committee. Survey undertaken by the County Social Crime Prevention Unit Coordinator.	Team located in premises independent of the three parent agencies (police, social services and probation). Composed of nine practitioners with administration assistance. The liaison structure of twice weekly meetings.

Points of comparison				
Referrals and assessment Referrals from education or social work. Assessor undertakes the information gathering task personally. *Work to support other professionals* Team works closely with other professionals involved with the child in order to negotiate common objectives. Goals are identified, discussed, prioritized. Roles and tasks are assigned. Face-to-face meetings with relevant people. *Feedback and networking* Feedback essential, if time consuming, to help professionals change their responses, attitudes, keep up to date and moving in the same direction.	*Referrals and assessment* Referrals made to locality teams from various sources including parents and self-referral by the young people. *Work to support other professionals* Enables professionals to develop their individual skills and enhance personal growth by working with other disciplines and using different tactics and strategies *Feedback and networking* Through the meetings structure and project organization. Includes young people. Positive feedback about young people's success encouraged at all points.	*Referrals and assessment* Whole age group involved. No desire to prove or disprove any particular theory. *Work to support other professionals* The findings provide useful information for service providers and shed light on issues of current interest to them. *Feedback and networking* A common base line of information was achieved via the report.	*Referrals and assessment* Majority of referrals offence based. Others from those seen to be 'at risk'. Information-gathering, assessment and decision-making is a joint process involving all relevant agencies. Strong emphasis on minimum intervention to avoid labelling. *Work to support other professionals* Team-based school liaison officers link with specific schools. Associated with large number of initiatives. Discussions about crime prevention work/attitude change. *Feedback and networking* Feedback to all the agencies concerning the problems and progress of young people. No formal network but every opportunity taken to take part in local debates in other forums.

Mobile Action Resource Service Project (MARS)

This project arose from concerns expressed by middle managers in Tayside social work and educational departments and the health board that some children seemed to 'proceed quickly through these services only to end up being removed from their families and/or schools' (Gulaboff 1989: 31). The project offered:

> direct work with children and families and a consultancy service to local professionals based on a comprehensive analysis of the child's situation, the perceptions held by key parties knowledge of the range of services involved. Emphasis is on clarifying short- and long-term objectives and securing the commitment of other professionals to these.
>
> (p. 30)

The project's objectives were:

1 To provide individualised programmes . . . to divert them from inappropriate residential care or removal from their community school or home.
2 To develop and promote working methods which
   (a) enable children and their families to remain together
   (b) facilitate children being cared for in the least institutionalised environment.
3 To challenge the process of labelling which tends to restrict the number of options available and identify the difficulties that arise between the agencies who do not share the same professional approaches, perspectives and recommendations.
4 To work alongside referring agencies in a sharing consultative role, with the purpose of jointly developing the best standards of practice.
5 To indicate to agencies how policy changes might promote the development of additional options, even within existing resources.

(p. 30)

The rationale for a multi-agency approach arose from a fear that 'the structure of our child welfare system may in itself generate fragmentation of a child's physical, emotional and social needs' (p. 35). Different agencies serving different needs did not necessarily take account of the interrelated nature of all the child's problems. Thus, the project held that 'Even when several agencies are involved, proper co-ordination and trust between agencies can overcome the dangers of fragmenting the services to the child and prevent any subsequent fragmentation of the child's personal life' (p. 35).

MARS's concept of an independent assessor was the model adopted by Elmore II for the inter-agency panel. The assessor undertook the information-gathering task personally, 'to develop a clear picture of the work that has been done and of the different perspectives of the family and other agencies' (Gulaboff 1989: 32). Although the term is not used, it is clear that independent assessors acted as network brokers. Their job was to:

identify inter-agency obstacles and misunderstandings which may have inadvertently hindered previous plans. We deliberately seek out what degree of commitment still exists to help the child. We interpret in a positive way what the other agencies tried to do and what were the constraints on them. We want to understand what changes they seek in the child's attitude or behaviour, no matter how trivial this seems.

(p. 32)

The team then identified and prioritized goals and assigned tasks. Although an inter-agency training role, other than consultancy for professionals working across agency boundaries, did not seem to be part of the project's brief, support for the professionals working with young people was regarded as important. MARS experienced the familiar catalogue of obstacles to effective inter-agency work: lack of time to meet colleagues in other agencies and ignorance of others' roles and responsibilities, leading to 'damaging stereotypes and the creation of a vicious circle of self fulfilling prophecies about the perceived intransigence of other agencies' (p. 36).

The team's belief was that if children were to improve, the professionals must be prepared to adapt. To help them, feedback, 'even seemingly insignificant information' (p. 35), especially to note successes, was essential, if time consuming. Regular feedback kept all professionals up to date and moving in the same direction. 'It is essential in this way to maintain the commitment of a multi-disciplinary team, especially when they are based in their own agencies' (p. 35). Plans made for the young people required 'a series of linked interventions and need careful and reliable co-ordination if they are to succeed. Separate tasks and objectives become more potent than just the sum of the parts, when linked across a network of people' (p. 33). Change in any part of the network, including the children and their families, needed to be reflected by changed responses elsewhere in the network.

Surrey Youth Link

Surrey Youth Link, in addition to strengthening existing links between schools and other agencies and creating new ones, sought to develop school-based projects for pupils outside normal school hours. Other projects to reduce vandalism in schools, to involve parents and the youth service and to promote social responsibility through curriculum development were also encouraged. In 1992, after the withdrawal of central government funding, Surrey County Council continued to support the project but expected it to extend multi-agency and multidisciplinary working and to support the Youth Link model in more schools. Joint funding with other agencies, particularly social services and the police, and the establishment of a clear management support structure were also priorities. The benefits of the model were that it 'identifies positive ways of helping disaffected pupils' to improve motivation, self-esteem and self-discipline, 'as opposed to options that increase alienation' (Surrey County Council 1992). The model was also designed to improve relationships between the student, family and school. The extra-curricular activities were designed for everyone 'but based on the targeted young people's needs, so that the influence of their peers on the young people is more effective.' Practitioners involved with the project reported that it helped them to appreciate the different professional roles played in relation to young people. It encouraged professionals such as education psychologists and education social workers (ESWs) to work in a different way in schools and to view young people targeted by the project in a more positive light.

Youth Link, managed by the youth service with the involvement of headteachers and their staff, had a committee structure consisting of:

- A county steering group (oversight of strategy and revenue).
- A Youth Link staff team 'to share good practice, discuss ideas or issues, monitor and evaluate the whole process and, when required, implement decisions made by the Steering Group'.
- Locality teams, 'the pivot of the model', were composed of a teacher/ coordinator, youth worker, education welfare officer and educational psychologist, and met weekly to monitor the progress of targeted pupils, take referrals, make decisions about the welfare of young people and liaise with school staff and other agencies as appropriate. It was regarded as important to identify from each discipline 'the right person with appropriate skills'. Young people were referred, or could self-refer, to the team, who then decided what help could be offered or arranged access to other agencies.
- Area support groups met termly, with all agencies invited to share concerns about individual young people.

Although feedback and networking were not emphasized strongly in project documentation, the meetings structure and project organization allowed these activities to take place. As with MARS, positive feedback about the success of young people previously regarded as 'difficult' was encouraged at all points.

Exeter Youth Support Team

The Exeter Youth Support Team's objective to divert juvenile offenders from the Criminal Justice System and the courts was achieved through the development of policies to prevent juvenile crime and to support a range of community-based initiatives such as Intermediate Treatment programmes. Team members believed that no one agency had exclusive knowledge, skills or experience in dealing with juvenile delinquency and that agencies might provide a more effective and consistent response were they to work together with shared aims and objectives. 'By having a focal point to which matters relating to juveniles can be referred, a co-ordinated response reflecting trends should emerge. This should enhance the policies of all the agencies involved ... In relation to policy development, it is important that decision making and working methods be based on research, rather than opinion or Agency prejudice' (Exeter Youth Support Team 1992). In the team's experience juvenile crime is mainly minor and transient, and court appearances tend to be followed by increases in delinquent activities, with all forms of intervention having a limited impact on offending behaviour. This was particularly true of custodial sentences and it was difficult to predict who will become delinquent. Thus the team were keen to maintain a broad perspective on the difficulties faced by young people and to support some services that were not exclusively reserved for offenders, such as work with girls and young women, and young people 'at risk' through housing difficulties. Feedback to all the agencies concerning the problems and progress of young people in the community seems to have achieved 'collaborative advantage' in what the team describes as 'the development of trust, co-operation and professional respect. This generates confidence in risk taking and in developing alternatives to prosecution, it also fosters credibility for the responses developed.' As a result, issues relating to crime prevention were discussed rather than individual cases. Developments such as the Community Assessment Group 'encourage the community to take responsibility for its youngsters in trouble, directly involving schools, families and other networks.'

Drawbacks of the model were thought to arise from 'the sophistication of services and the availability of resources'. Children can get drawn into these and become labelled. In addition, 'an inter-agency team could be accused of collusion'. To counter this the team stressed the importance of clear roles, responsibilities and duties along agency lines which provide demarcation. 'While working to common aims and objectives, our individual perspectives inevitably differ, allowing for discussion and inter-professional debates.'

Mid Glamorgan Multi-agency and Multi-disciplinary Partnership Project

This project differed from the previous three in that it did not focus on case work. Instead, it was set up to address what would now be regarded as a 'wicked issue': an intractable problem, too complex for any one agency or organization to deal with in isolation. In this case the issue was crime, alcohol and substance abuse. National and local surveys during the 1980s showed that 'Mid Glamorgan is one of the poorest and most deprived areas in Britain', with high levels of unemployment, poor housing, high death rates and proportion of residents off sick (Mid Glamorgan Social Crime Prevention Unit c.1992). There was particular concern, in relation to health, about the lifestyles of young people in the county. To tackle these problems, three multi-agency committees were formed to develop a common baseline of information. Simple pooling of existing agency data was not possible because data were insufficient, incompatible or inappropriate. The project carried out a survey of over 13,000 young people at school in Mid Glamorgan 'to improve mutual understanding of young people and together develop policies, resources and services which are appropriate and responsive to the needs of young people in Mid Glamorgan during the 1990s.' A multi-agency survey steering committee 'provided a pool of expert information, or access to information, from every profession, discipline and agency in Mid Glamorgan.' The planning, coordination and action in connection with the survey was undertaken by the County Social Crime Prevention Unit Coordinator. Fifty-eight per cent of all school attenders aged 13–18 years in 42 schools responded.

There are a number of points of comparison between this project and Elmore II. First, the objective was to gain insights into young people's views on issues of concern to the agencies and organizations involved. This was achieved by asking the young people themselves. Second, the organizers did not want to prove or disprove any particular theory. 'The clearly stated intention was to mount a simple exploratory and descriptive investigation which would raise questions about the development of service delivery and practice.' This approach revealed that concern about alcohol and drug use and abuse was an overreaction by social welfare and law enforcement agencies. The findings highlighted instead the lack of social activities for young people, with crime appearing to be a 'social event' and criminal activity 'a sort of moral holiday'. The report suggested that one effective crime prevention strategy would be to make organized youth leisure activities more appealing to the crime-prone 14–16-year-old age group.

Characteristics of good practice

Comparison of these projects with each other and with Elmore II suggests that children and young people, when asked about their problems and what would improve their lives, raise upstream preventative, environmental issues stressing their rights as citizens. Agencies, on the other hand, appear to focus on downstream problems and the legislative, organizational, financial and professional practice obstacles standing in the way of inter-agency cooperation. Effective inter-agency cooperation should, it seems, be directed more firmly towards improving the quality of young people's lives in general, as we see happening ten years on, in initiatives such as Sure Start.

Although improved inter-agency cooperation is required to carry out effective downstream work with individuals, a proportion of this effort, these projects seem to suggest, should be used to identify characteristics of good practice which can be used to benefit everyone. This analysis would explain the marked unwillingness expressed by all the projects discussed here to categorize, label or otherwise compartmentalize young people regarded as 'at risk': to do so would have impeded downstream work and obscured upstream options. This also makes sense of the emphasis in these projects on networking, feedback and the inter-personal skills required to effect change: 'the right person with appropriate skills' (Surrey County Council 1992). What is interesting is the question of how successfully upstream and downstream work can be integrated. It is claimed here that downstream work is important for two reasons – lives and life chances may be saved that would otherwise be lost, and lessons are learnt which can feed into upstream endeavour. We have as yet limited experience of large-scale upstream inter-agency work, though practice is developing fast in the new climate of support for it. An important indication of success will be the continued willingness to learn from the experience of the most marginalized and vulnerable. The independent assessor acted as the scout out on the margins for Elmore II and MARS. It seems that the small-scale local project for 'through the net' children is needed to play the same role for the big upstream initiatives. Indeed, an examination of the role of the personal advisors employed by Connexions suggests that they need the support of just such groups (DfEE 2001). Without them, they are no more likely to succeed with TTN young people than their predecessors working within agency boundaries.

Despite the small number of comparable inter-agency projects available during this important transition period, it was, nonetheless, possible to identify characteristics of good inter-agency practice. These were identified as:

- formal commitment and support from senior management and from political to practitioner level;
- formal and regular inter-agency meetings to discuss ethical issues, changes in legislation and practice, gaps in provision and information-sharing at all levels to develop short- and long-term strategies;
- common work practices in relation to legislation, referral/assessment, joint vocabulary, agreed definitions, procedures and outcomes;
- common agreement of client group and collective ownership of the problems, leading to early intervention;
- mechanisms for exchange of confidential information;
- a framework for collecting data and statistical information across all agencies that can inform all practice, including ethnic monitoring;
- monitoring and evaluation of services in relation to inter-agency work;
- joint training in order to understand each other's professional role (Roaf and Lloyd 1995).

As with the factors identified by Elmore II, these characteristics reflect concerns about legislation, strategy and organizational and professional practice. They reinforce the connection between systemic and process factors noted earlier, and the interplay of upstream and downstream work. One would expect these features also to characterize effective children's services plans. Atkinson *et al.* (2001), in an audit of multi-agency working, list key factors in success which identify a similar range of features, with, as one might expect in the current climate, a much more explicit reference to funding and resource issues.

Youth strategy and children's services plans

Children's services plans, originally recommended in the Utting Report (1991), did not become mandatory until 1997. They were intended to be multi-agency, with local authorities consulting a wide range of agencies and voluntary organizations. In the present context they can be viewed as a means of introducing inter-agency meta-strategy, backed with the force of law. Implementation depends to an extent on local interpretation, which varies according to local tradition, agency culture and local values and commitment to children and young people. In Scotland, regional councils, such as Lothian and Strathclyde, began moving in this direction in the early 1980s, at least ten years ahead of their English counterparts.

Lothian Youth Strategy

Lothian Youth Strategy was adopted by the then minority Conservative administration in 1983. It aimed to 'cope with some of the region's most difficult youngsters' (Maginnis 1989: 7) and was based on four principles:

1 Problems associated with children's behaviour or circumstances should be dealt with wherever possible by keeping the child in his or her local community, using the resources of the family and other local resources in a flexible manner.
2 Children who are at risk of having to leave home, who are at risk of being excluded from school or who have special educational need should be jointly assessed and in some cases jointly reviewed.
3 Both the education and social work departments will endeavour to contribute day and group work provision as an alternative to the residential care of adolescent children where this is appropriate.
4 No child should be recommended for residential care unless:
   (a) he or she has no home (including a substitute home) in the community which can, with appropriate support, provide an adequate degree of control or care, or
   (b) he or she is at risk to himself/herself or others in the community, or
   (c) he or she has medical, psychiatric or special educational needs which can only be dealt with in a residential context, and/or it is in the child's best interest which cannot be met in any other way (p. 7).

These principles marked Lothian's first public commitment 'to the concepts of community based resources and joint co-operation between the education and social work departments to resolve the difficulties of the adolescent youngster with emotional and behavioural difficulties.' As Maginnis, a local councillor at the time, points out, these principles could have remained as a paper exercise only. In 1983, implementation was left in the hands of council officers working in a highly complex and hierarchical bureaucratic system of management.

The fact that the youth strategy survived is attributed to the quality of the concept and the belief of a number of officers in its principles. They recommended ways in which to implement the strategy, in which the children's hearing system played a key role. The various consultative groups set up by the hearing system to encourage liaison between themselves and the regional council put pressure on the social work department. Meanwhile, panel members, concerned about truancy, brought pressure to bear on the education system. The result was that in 1987 the newly appointed Labour administration, acting on the recommendation of the children's panel policy planning committee, set up a youth strategy subcommittee. This group quickly found that to achieve the 'fundamental change necessary to make the strategy real and effective we were going to have to . . . set about shifting attitudes, changing work practices, and encouraging innovation . . . It would have to be plainly demonstrated that professionals . . . were accountable to the strategy. Uproar followed' (Maginnis 1989: 9). In overcoming local resistance, Maginnis records the support provided by Barnardo's, which, in support of the principles of the Youth Strategy, closed down an 'out of region' residential school for primary age children and diverted funds to the local strategy.

In implementing the strategy Lothian recognized that the task was to secure collaborative advantage. Departments would have to be persuaded to see the professional advantage to themselves and the young people of pursuing a strategy which required cooperation and joint action. Youth strategy must, therefore, 'have a management structure which recognises and allows for the significant differences in philosophy, training and attitudes which exist among all professional participants in the strategy' (Maginnis 1989: 10). The committee concluded that the lead role in implementation should be taken by education, on the grounds that schools saw children every day: 'So it makes sense that the local authority's strategy, designed to meet the needs of every child at risk or in difficulty, should be centred on the service most likely to be encountering the child on a daily basis' (p. 11). This was the approach advocated, though never implemented, by Kilbrandon (1964) and contrasts with the lead role given to social services departments by the 1989 Children Act.

In practical terms, the strategy was supported by a range of initiatives, including individual counselling, group work with families and specialized resources and facilities for children and young people with acute needs. From the beginning, a key element in the strategy was the intention that all secondary schools should establish school liaison groups (SLGs), for which detailed guidelines were provided (Lothian Regional Council 1992). An SLG operates as a local inter-agency forum 'able to intervene at the earliest opportunity to support a child experiencing difficulties by drawing on the best amalgam of joint professional skills and resources' (Maginnis 1989: 11). Before a young person could be excluded, for example, it was recommended that he or she should be the subject of a joint assessment by the SLG. A key objective was to free professionals from concentrating all their energies on case work, without considering the broader, societal issues involved.

The second report on the work of SLGs (Lothian Regional Council 1991) records that about 2 per cent of the region's secondary school population had been referred during the year and that the strategy 'is making a major contribution to these young people and their families through the inter-agency forum of the SLG' (p. 16). The report speaks of 'a creative array of support intervention' (p. 17) and schools were reported to be making good use of the inter-agency forum provided by SLGs. School staff were more aware of SLGs and their purpose, and of the contribution they could make to school policy-making and in-service training.

Ultimately, the creators of Lothian's Youth Strategy hoped for 'a sense of community responsibility where every agency and professional shares the common objective of care and progress, for every child' (Lothian Regional Council 1991: 14). After local government reorganization, the strategy remained intact in terms of basic principles and policy, but was reshaped under the title 'Working Together' (City of Edinburgh Council 1997).

Inter-agency work in transition

Two recent initiatives are discussed briefly here, the first as an example of joining up services in an English local authority, the second showing the development of an inter-agency project in a rural area.

Hertfordshire Service for Children, Schools and Families

After more than two years of planning, development and consultation, within the government's Quality Protects programme, Hertfordshire introduced its new service for children, schools and families in April 2001. As an organization created by the integration of the previously separate education services and social services, its rationale is to improve support for all children and to provide a more coordinated approach which puts the child at the centre. Although it will take some while for the new service to develop its full potential, there are some similarities and points of contrast with Lothian's development of youth strategy 15 years earlier. The shift in perspective over these years in relation to children is marked. Thus the four principles of Lothian's strategy focus on children's difficulties, while Hertfordshire's focus on the development of an inclusive service bringing agencies together to make universal provision, with preventative work 'a central aspect . . . finding ways of stopping problems arising' (Hertfordshire County Council 2001). An emphasis on the development of a unified casework system, with schools able to refer individuals to a dedicated case worker, is likely to have done much to reassure schools during the transition to the new service. It will be interesting to see how support for this role develops and whether, coupled with the further preventative strategies proposed, this reduces the number of those at risk of falling 'through the net'. Finding new ways to encourage agencies and professionals to overcome differences in agency and professional culture and approach to clients was as much concern to Lothian in the 1980s as it is to Hertfordshire today: training, including joint training, for inter-agency work in initial and post-experience professional training thus continues to be an issue despite the lapse of time. It will also be interesting to see what coordinating structures will develop in the wake of joined up meta-strategy, possibly with school based inter-agency meetings such as those described by Lloyd et al. (2001) in Scotland and Elmore-type inter-agency teams and networks. Hertfordshire's example repeated, more widely, would also bring a new dimension to the debate over how government departments can become more effectively coordinated.

Thame Area Children and Young Persons' Network (Elmore III)

This project set out to adapt the Elmore model to suit a rural area 15 miles from central services in Oxford. Practitioners formed an inter-agency network in 1996, to support each other in making a more coherent response to the needs of vulnerable young people in the area. A grant from the Calouste Gulbenkian Foundation led to the setting up of an inter-agency steering group. The headteachers of the local partnership of secondary school and feeder primary schools took responsibility for overall project strategy and funding. A proportion of the grant was spent on low-cost pump priming projects identified via the network, producing a local directory of resources, organizing inter-agency training for learning support assistants and creating a therapy access fund to help children access prescribed therapy. The fund paid for taxi fares from the villages to therapy provision in Thame, or for child care for younger siblings, where no family support network was available.

Family–School–Community links worker

The balance of the grant was spent on a new project, again identified by the network, to promote:

- Pupil support and learning: work with identified children at times of change (bereavement, family distress) or transfer (moving from primary to secondary and post-16).
- Training: to suggest improvements schools might make to reduce the effect of change on children's achievement, and extend peer mentoring.
- Support for parents and teachers concerned about the emotional and behavioural difficulties of children.
- Successful inter-agency practice – train LSAs as family–school–community links workers and provide further inter-agency training opportunities.

A part-time para-professional was appointed to further these objectives. Day-to-day support was provided by a school counsellor, with additional input from social worker, educational social worker and health visitor. The work involved liaison with education, health, social services and the youth service, taking referrals from parents, school and school nurse and making home visits where needed. As a para-professional with strong professional support, the worker was able to cross county boundaries where an agency professional could not and was also able to form relationships with families where professionals might have felt compromised. By the end of the pilot period, the schools were willing to share the cost of the worker's continued employment, with social services also contributing.

Although Elmore III had developed its own way of working in response to local conditions and therefore differed in some respects from Elmore I and II, it resembled them in structure and in the roles needed to maintain it. It had successfully identified gaps in provision and found ways to address these. The network had built trust between practitioners from a range of agencies and encouraged them to feed creative solutions into their systems and processes. One of these was to experiment with a new inter-agency role, the family–school–community links worker, for whom, as a para-professional, inter-agency barriers did not seem to exist. Administrative boundaries and remoteness from the centre, on the other hand, effectively blocked communication pathways, particularly to health services. The absence of an inter-agency strategy group for the locality was very important in terms of support for its ideas and for financial security, but had the unexpected benefit of linking the project much more closely to its community through its schools and its young people.

Conclusion

The projects and strategies outlined in this chapter cover the transition period discussed above. In the early 1990s, inter-agency projects record a sense of innovation. Projects were short-term, multi-agency, team-based 'pilots', funded from charitable sources directed at specific groups, frequently young offenders or young people in care. Very few could be found that focused on agency cooperation in relation to children and young people defined in a manner which stressed the social and environmental factors that put them 'at risk' or 'in difficulty', and that could not be resolved by short-term attention to individual need. Long-term strategies were also required. Lothian, Mid Glamorgan and, very recently, Hertfordshire are examples of local authority attempts to achieve this, while Exeter Youth Support Team, MARS and Surrey Youth Link display this philosophy in the context of their more specifically case management focused projects.

Second, it was not always easy to establish the organizational structure of a project. Those which had been taken on by local authorities tended to have developed organizational structures at senior and middle management levels linking them into the agencies they served, rather than being part of an overall inter-agency meta-strategy for children and young people, which in any event, did not appear to exist. In informal discussions held with inter-agency project leaders, it seemed that of the three elements of the inter-agency coordinating model identified in Elmore II, the element most frequently absent was the practitioner-based network. This was important given that the network was the least expensive element of the model, and most effective in terms of feedback. Sometimes a network existed but its significance was ignored or undervalued. In most of the projects discussed, feedback and networking are implied rather than specifically catered for and few strategies were used to develop and promote their benefits. Information sharing was invariably informal, unless, as in the example from Mid Glamorgan, taking place in the wake of a major survey. Strategies such as newsletters, fact files or directories of local resources, for sharing and discussing ideas, concepts and local issues, were not much in evidence. The significance and operation of networks is, indeed, only recently being fully analysed (McCabe *et al.* 1997; Wilson and Charlton 1997).

Finally, evaluative frameworks for inter-agency initiatives have yet to be devised (Lewis and Utting 2001). The history of inter-agency work suggests that these are only beginning to be considered and that much depends on the perspective of childhood and adolescence that is adopted. Hodgkin and Newell's (1996) review of effective government structures for children emphasizes that the perspectives on children governing such structures require elaboration and wider discussion before evaluative frameworks can be developed. A strength of the model of coordination emerging from the evidence of Elmore II, and the other projects studied, is its potential as an evaluative framework. For all these reasons, the conclusions reached by Elmore II still appeared to hold:

1 A formal structure promoting inter-agency collaboration would encourage agencies to innovate and to provide a fully coordinated service for young people needing more support than can be provided by any one of them.
2 Although the nature of the problems identified is complex and involves large agencies in change, effective and innovative solutions can emanate from small-scale inexpensive inter-agency projects (Roaf and Lloyd 1995).

The next chapter considers how such a framework can be further developed.

CHAPTER SIX

Building coordination: the interaction of system and process

Elmore I set out to improve inter-agency practice in relation to 'difficult to place' adults and had achieved some success through the innovative work of the ECST. 'The Network', known and used by everyone involved with DTP adults locally, had been in place since the early 1980s and the ECST was its brainchild. With the existence of an interdependent team and network, an inter-agency structure was beginning to take shape. Thus when practitioners got together to replicate the work of Elmore I for the benefit of TTN children and young people, they were also aware that they might be introducing not just a free-standing project, but a whole new structure, into the local agency scene and that this could be problematic. The need for improvements in inter-agency cooperation might be acknowledged, but why, it was argued, was a new structure needed? Could improvements in inter-agency practice not be achieved through existing agency channels? This was a difficult question to answer since, at that stage, the model emerging was still shadowy and not fully understood. Moreover, the proliferation of agencies and inter-agency agencies which has taken place post-1997 was still some way off and inter-agency working was by no means as widely accepted as it is now. This chapter looks at how these ideas became more explicit. It starts by considering the problems of agencies and young people identified in Elmore II and the implications of these for the larger role now assumed for inter-agency work in statutory and non-statutory services.

Analysis of the problems (see pp. 68–70) experienced by the young people and the agencies involved with them showed that these fell into four main groups, within which it is possible to identify factors contributing to success. These factors are also reflected in the characteristics of successful practice identified by other small-scale inter-agency projects operating at the time (see Chapter 5).

Factors influencing the progress of inter-agency work

Legislation

In Elmore II, although very few of the problems identified by agencies related directly to legislation, its effects were regarded as critical. Legislators had reinforced agency boundaries and offered few solutions other than exhortation to overcome them. The young people mentioned legislation tangentially in terms of ignorance of their rights under existing legislation. This was particularly noted in relation to ethnic minority groups, to girls and to those with mental health problems.

Despite many recommendations in government reports, only rarely had structures been built into the legislation to ensure that coordination took place. Without this safeguard, local attempts to improve coordination were easily frustrated. Rarely, for example, was there any one agency, team or service which would take responsibility for coordinating services for vulnerable young people, to support those who slip through existing provision and guide them back to it. Legislation was conflicting in its implications for children, with many different agencies sharing different responsibilities for young people, and this became more problematic post-16. These factors in combination made it difficult to coordinate provision or to develop a holistic care plan for a young person.

The missed opportunity, provided by the 1989 Children Act, to agree on common definitions meant that 'need' was defined in a different way in each agency. This constrained them from developing more inclusive practice and impacted on how different statutory responsibilities in relation to children and young people were interpreted. The requirement in the 1989 Children Act (Section 1) that 'the child's welfare should be the court's paramount consideration' and that a court 'shall have regard in particular to the ascertainable wishes and feelings of the child' was largely disregarded in education legislation for young people post-16. In the 1994 Code of Practice on the identification and assessment of special educational needs this requirement comes a poor second to the regard expressed for the wishes of parents. Little progress had been made in promoting child impact statements, which, it was proposed in the late 1980s, should be attached to legislation (Freeman 1987). These still have to be called for rather than legislated for (Cohen and Long 1998; Hancox 1999). In the mid-1990s, Parsons *et al.* (1994: 50), in their report on excluded primary school children, conclude that 'The law as it stands at present is inadequate to protect the educational rights of behaviourally difficult children who come to be excluded from school.' This is still an issue.

This state of affairs is all the more frustrating in that some aspects of past legislation, such as the 1969 Children and Young Person's Act, the 1973 National Health Service Re-organisation Act and the 1981 Education Act, had been enabling in terms of inter-agency work. Legislation has always been regarded as a key factor in either hindering or supporting inter-agency cooperation. The stumbling block, however, has been the failure to legislate across government departments to provide the framework to support inter-agency coordination. This failure particularly inhibited the joint planning and joint financial arrangements necessary to resource inter-agency collaboration, points made forcefully by the Audit Commission (1994, 1996), and left a vacuum rapidly filled with uncoordinated inter-agency activity and small-scale action research projects supported by the voluntary sector.

Strategic and organizational matters

About one-third of the problems (see pp. 68–70) identified by Elmore II in relation to agencies and one-half of those identified in relation to the young people could be directly linked to the way in which agencies were organized. Young people were categorized by agency boundary rather than an analysis of their needs. They were thus all too readily, and sometimes inappropriately, compartmentalized. They might, for example, receive help if they were seen as eligible for a truancy programme fronted by education, but if they became homeless or left school, then they fell 'through the net' again. Collaboration across agencies was difficult in the absence of strategic planning across agencies and with responsibility for service delivery frequently managed vertically within agencies.

Since there was no organized means of communication, and still less collaboration with another agency, practitioners did not know which agency to turn to if their own agency could no longer help. If they were committed to helping their clients, they did what they could on their own or referred only to agencies or professionals with whom they were already familiar. As a consequence, practitioners became confused about the limits of their professional responsibility. In general the effect was for practitioners to spend too much time working on their own with young people in difficulties and too little time in cooperation with others to make joint plans. Thus, when young people, particularly older teenagers, fell 'through the net', it was no one's responsibility to bring them back. Agencies therefore had difficulty in seeing 'cases' through the 'system'. Similarly, there was little coordinated help available when a young person transferred from one school to another, or was permanently excluded from school, or moved in or out of care, or from pre- to post-16 provision (Fletcher-Campbell 1997). Nor were the consequences of this brought home unless there was a crisis, possibly resulting in media attention and adverse publicity for whichever agency or individual front-line worker was thought to be at fault at the time.

Financial arrangements

The lack of effective joint funding mechanisms, like legislation, is implied in the list of problems faced by agencies. Although it was frequently invoked, informally, as a reason for not embarking on inter-agency activity, sometimes this seemed to be an avoidance strategy. Problems were compounded because local and national government and agencies faced competing claims for, usually, decreasing funds and it was not always clear whether funding priorities were for family services or for children's services.

Even where local inter-agency funding strategies existed, such as joint commissioning, these could easily get bogged down in debates about which group of children to prioritize and were not helped by different agency perceptions and definitions of 'need'. Kendrick *et al.* (1996: 30) found that 'even within the same local authority, defensiveness about departmental budgets has created major tensions, particularly in relation to education and social work . . . joint commissioning and multi-funding of services will be essential.' Other initiatives, such as local financial management of schools, had effectively dispersed LEA budgets. LEAs had, as a consequence, lost the ability to vire money from one spending head to another and were also denied access to the, sometimes, large sums held in school balances (Audit Commission 1993).

Huffington and Brunning (1994: 10) comment that:

Public sector organizations are now more tightly managed on a local basis and the purchaser/provider model is being adapted across the board. This brings with it notions of increased responsiveness to the consumers' needs and service quality. Both concepts concern the creation of feed back loops between consumers and providers of services so as to create the most effective services to meet needs. Local knowledge is highly valued in this culture . . . Team work and inter-agency co-operation are, however, being stressed to ensure that the services are bought and cost effectiveness is maximised.

Parsons *et al.* (1994: 41) found that 'costing public services, and more particularly child care services, is a relatively recent development.' Improved liaison and less cost shunting was resting, the study found, on the unsure foundation of good personal relations rather than formalized procedures.

Professional practice

Nearly half of the agency problems uncovered by Elmore II appeared to arise from matters concerning professional relationships or working methods, with little understanding of what inter-agency work meant in terms of skills and practice. Different methods of assessment and gate-keeping devices controlling access to resources and different attitudes towards confidentiality were frequently mentioned as stumbling blocks. There were persistent problems of communication and few opportunities for policy-makers and practitioners to meet on equal terms. Yet given the interest over the past thirty years in the application of psychological theory and of general systems theory to organizations of all kinds and to human relationships in the workplace, the frustration caused by the blocked arteries of communication was less easily tolerated than formerly. Thomas (1992: 63) suggests that there may now be a greater willingness on the part of the institution as a whole to changes which reflect 'negotiations among participants in complex networks'. Elmore II's purpose, with the research officer acting as the project's probe, or scout, was to explore and fully participate in these negotiations at the interface between agencies. It transpired that what were required there, apart from credibility as a fellow professional, were inter-personal and inter-professional skills. What are these? Can they be broken down into abilities which can then be specifically written down in a job description? The study of inter-agency projects suggests a strong association between effective inter-professional/inter-agency skills and inter-personal skills.

Inter-personal skills as a core competency for inter-agency work

Developments in social psychology and systemic work with organizations help to explain some of the difficulties experienced by practitioners in their relationships with colleagues in their own and other agencies. Elmore II uncovered a number of perspectives and ways of construing among practitioners and researchers. According to Campbell *et al.* (1994: 2):

1 When people think systemically, they are able to understand better the effects of connectedness in organizations, and account more effectively for the dilemmas and tensions that arise during change.
2 When people understand and accept how they collectively create and maintain a mental picture of the organization and its problems they are able to alter and renegotiate these understandings and find new ways of solving their problems.

The ability to 'think systemically' suggests flexibility and sensitivity of mind, and willingness to change and adapt, even under pressure and when stressed. To facilitate this ability in others suggests that interpersonal skills are also required, to help, for example, a team or individual to reframe problems in ways which admit of change and solution. Campbell *et al.* (1989: 2) imply as much:

> We believe that organizations change when people's perception of beliefs and behaviour changes. Our understanding of the organization allows us to have conversations which lead people to make that change . . . As we share our observations we come to an understanding of the meaning these beliefs and relationships have for the larger organization. Through this process, beliefs and relationships are seen in different ways and alternative actions can be devised.

The literature on inter-agency working in human services provision relating to children and young people, corroborated by work on inter-organizational collaboration in the world of business management, suggests that inter- and intra-personal skills do, in fact, form the core of inter-professional competencies. This is reflected in Elmore II's finding that:

> Where conflicts arise [between agencies] these are often attributed to personalities and individual agency difficulties rather than to the lack of a structure which would support and validate collaboration. There is

little perception that effective joint working might alleviate the problems of the agencies as well as those of the young people.

(Roaf and Lloyd 1995)

Thus structure and process are inextricably linked and shortcomings in either
lead to dysfunctional professional and agency behaviour. The 'connecting
tissue', so to speak, is to be found in the area of inter-personal skills. To what
extent (to introduce another metaphor into an already metaphor-laden story)
do inter-personal skills play the part of the pedals between the structure and
process wheels of the inter-agency bicycle?

In the early 1990s, practitioners could not yet deal openly with the frustration caused by inter-personal difficulties, yet the need to do so was becoming
more urgent as the move towards social inclusion gathered pace. Thomas
(1992) considers the introduction into mainstream classrooms of adults other
than teachers, a response to the increasing numbers of children with special
needs, previously marginalized in special schools. In the microcosm of the
classroom, study of the inter-personal relationships between teachers and
their aides suggested that there are 'mismatches or tensions which impede the
effectiveness of teams', which may be 'managerial, interpersonal, ideological,
definitional, practical or personal' (Thomas 1992: 53).

Inter-personal skills, as a key component of effective inter-agency cooperation, have not been an easy area to discuss, and ground rules based on coherent
theory and practice have yet to develop. In Elmore II, steering group members had to make up their own guidelines for what would be regarded as
good inter-agency behaviour and these were not easy to adhere to. The idea
that inter-professional competencies can be identified and that inter-personal
skills are a core skill and can be taught is likewise relatively new, though
increasingly acknowledged. Wilson and Charlton (1997: 49), in their guide
for the development of partnership in the public, private, voluntary and
community sectors, consider that 'Interpersonal skills are the secret weapon
of a successful partnership management process':

One cannot ignore the importance of interpersonal skills in any management process. These are skills which can be taught and can be
acquired . . . But skills cannot be bolted on where there is no willingness
to be open about one's own position or to the different views of others.

(p. 50)

Some light is shed on the nature of these skills by Huffington and Brunning
(1994) in their edition of essays by 'internal consultants' in the public sector. Internal consultancy, they suggest, is being increasingly used to bring
about change, partly because it is cheaper, but chiefly because the internal
consultant 'is more knowledgeable about the system, more aware of local
particularities' (Huffington and Brunning 1994: Foreword). Furthermore,
internal consultants:

are part of the system they observe, which also experiences them . . . Those
who truly understand their system dynamics use not their own power

but the force-fields in the system itself. The idea is to use minimalist interventions to achieve optimal results. It is this that vindicates the skill of the system dynamicist.

(Foreword)

In playing this role, 'a consultant enters into a relationship with a client – whether an individual, group or an organization – about a work related issue broader than the management of an individual case' (p. 2). Network brokers, it would appear from this description, are 'system dynamicists'.

However, Campbell *et al.* (1994: 49) counsel against an oversimplistic approach to 'core competencies'. They found that the components of management skills were more generally focused on 'doing' – for example, negotiating, appraising – with little attention given to 'the contextual or relational aspects of these skills'. In their view, 'competencies describe *behaviour in relationships*, not behaviour in isolation. Thus competencies are mental constructs, things that arise through a process of negotiation and agreement between people' (p. 49). Fenichel and Eggbeer's (1990) aphoristic description of the skills required for inter-agency working as 'the ability to do the right thing, at the right time, for the right reason' suggests inter-professional and inter-personal skills of a high order.

Building a framework for communication and feedback

Studies of the problems facing agencies and young people suggested that they could be further reduced to two groups: systems and process. Past history, going back to the examples of the Scottish Children's Hearing, the multiprofessional assessment process for children with special educational needs and the Working Together protocols to prevent child abuse, as well as many exhortations from the time of the Warnock Report (1978) to more recent reports from the Audit Commission (1994, 1996), emphasized the importance of coordination. Looked at in this way, it became clear that the most important contribution of the three-tier coordinating structure emerging from the work of Elmore I and II was to provide a communication system for all those involved in any way with their DTP and TTN client groups. However, it was a structure which could easily become dysfunctional. If, for example, any element was missing, or if use of the system was undermined or undervalued, communication processes broke down. Thus if either structure or process became dysfunctional the risks to the client group would increase. Conversely, in a well maintained structure risks could be expected to decrease. As an analogy, the structure resembled the human body, with head, body and nervous system: effective coordination requires all three to function well.

In Elmore I, the support team and network were the most visible elements. Practitioners with appropriate professional skills were either seconded or employed in their own right to combine their expertise in the team and to assess and case manage those with complex and multiple needs. This involved 'network-broking' around the agencies, either to return the client to the appropriate agency or to identify elements in a flexible package of support which combined the resources of a number of agencies. This was a task for a small inter-agency team of practitioners supervised by an inter-agency steering group. The policy- or strategy-making element was shadowy. In fact, looked at again systemically and with hindsight, the role of the chair of the steering group was to act as a 'high-level', informal network broker among what came to be known within the group as 'the top brass' – heads of service to be reckoned with but rarely seen. Since the project was, at that stage, self-funding, the existence of the ECST presented few problems for policy-makers. By contrast, in the case of Elmore II a few years later, funding for public services challenged 'the top brass' in a way which no amount of network-broking by middle managers could overcome. For Elmore II, policy-makers were no longer shadowy and the policy-making element was revealed as a third crucial element in the structure.

There may have been other factors, apart from funding, which made cooperation and hence coordination difficult to achieve, especially at the policy-making level. Children, as Hornby (1993) points out, are at the centre of different discourses and different domains and have more professionals involved with them than any other group. Some important differences between TTN children and young people and DTP adults were noted by members of both Elmore I and II. Agency boundaries, they thought, were fairly clear in the case of the adults, and disputes were about gaps, whereas with children, these boundaries were less distinct. There were fewer gaps but the overlap in responsibility was an issue because children, unlike adults, were never out of someone's responsibility, though much depended on the agency mandate. Moreover, however challenging and difficult agencies might find children, their response was likely to be more optimistic. In the case of 'difficult to place' adults, agencies might be happier to let go since their clients were not always perceived as 'attractive' or as having much going for them. Children, on the other hand, attract loyalty from those who work with them and individual agencies can be correspondingly keen to hang on to them even if they cannot, on their own, provide a full package of care. No agency wants to admit failure with children and one of the major achievements of the past ten years has been that so many practitioners and policy-makers now see cooperative working as a sign of strength, not weakness.

However, to use Huxham and Macdonald's (1992) terminology, the policy-making element at senior management level was needed because at no other level could 'meta-strategy' be devised to secure 'collaborative advantage'. Significantly, Elmore II straddles the period between 1991, the year in which the 1989 Children Act was implemented, and 1997, when children's services plans became mandatory. The model proposed by Elmore II was designed, therefore, at a time when inter-agency strategy was still in the melting pot, and needs to be viewed as such. Having undertaken from the start to resist the temptation to attribute problems of collaboration to personalities and individual agency difficulties, the project turned its attention instead to structural reasons for these problems (Roaf and Lloyd 1995). Once a structure had been identified it became easier to understand how structure and process could interact positively to create the effective communication system that young people at risk of falling 'through the net' appeared to need. The basic outline of the structure is to be found in Figure 6.1. The key activities associated with each level are listed below, suggesting the range of benefits each element might bring to agencies and to individual TTN young people.

The senior management policy and planning group:
- develops good practice arising from initiatives in existence and proposed;
- ensures the funding and development of initiatives, monitoring and evaluation;
- supports research (e.g. into the mental health needs of young people);
- determines future policy locally;
- oversees the management, monitoring and evaluation of the support team(s)/panel(s).

The middle management team:
- works with all agencies to ensure that an individual is appropriately maintained within the care system;
- acts as a network broker for all agencies, statutory and non-statutory, to secure appropriate support for individual children and young people, taking responsibility, and providing a key worker for a case if necessary;
- acts as a catalyst promoting inter-agency cooperation and developing flexible packages of support for individual children and young people within existing agencies;
- suggests suitable areas for research and development for the consideration of the policy group;
- develops materials and creates training opportunities for those working across agency boundaries.

For *agencies*, the team/panel:
- extends the work each agency can undertake with young people that tax it;
- clarifies and justifies the boundaries of all service providers;
- provides flexible packages of support when long-term intervention and continuity are required;
- provides independent assessors for the cases referred to the team/panel;
- supports existing case/key workers within agencies;
- promotes networking and collaboration between agencies, encouraging them to extend their remit;
- provides a resource able to move flexibly between agencies as gaps in provision arise and are filled;
- works with others to build additional resources (for example to negotiate for funding and staffing);
- provides a 'minder' (see Chapter 7) for the 'Network'.

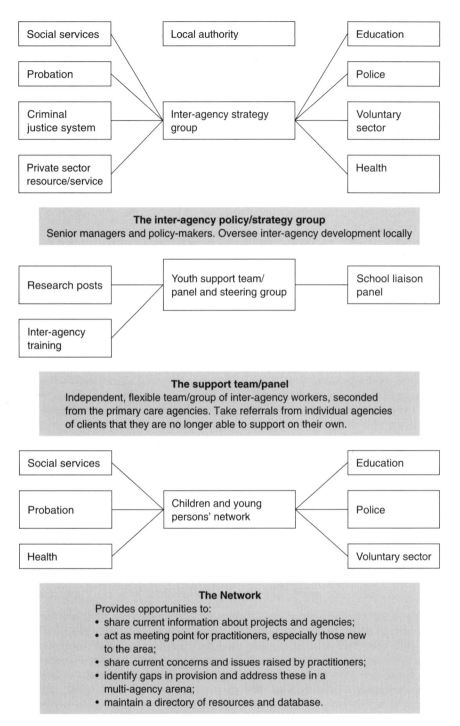

Figure 6.1 Inter-agency coordinating structures

For *individual children and young people* the team/panel:
- provides long-term continuity and support by allocating a key worker in cases where such a person cannot be identified from existing agencies;
- arranges flexible packages of support appropriate to clients' short- and long-term needs, enabling them to remain in, or return to, the network of existing provision.

The *network* collectively:
- formalizes informal networks;
- enables the group to focus on achievable aims;
- enables reciprocity in co-working relationships;
- offers an opportunity to challenge and influence the philosophies and procedures of others;
- preserves group autonomy, while enhancing partnership;
- improves services for clients because of better contacts and local knowledge;
- helps agency key workers to manage client problems by creating an extended team supportive of each other and sensitive to needs;
- identifies gaps in services which are likely to be responded to best through partnership.

The structure provides a coherent whole through which information sharing, research, training and policy-making can all be coordinated in a manner which guarantees that client needs can, if necessary, be addressed independently of those of the professionals and agencies. Agency and client difficulties are given parity of concern and professionals in difficulties are not compromised. The structure allows information and feedback to be focused and channelled positively and formally through the system, rather than being dissipated in individual informal conversation elsewhere.

A model such as this serves a useful purpose as a training tool by helping individuals or groups to identify the current structures within which they operate and to locate themselves in that structure. Practitioners can identify which elements of the model exist already in their area and which need to be developed. The model is useful when:

- an individual, group, agency or agencies begin to plan activities to improve practice in relation to an identified client group;
- explaining the importance of a structured approach to inter-agency cooperation;
- demonstrating the worth of every person involved with the client group.

In this model front-line workers are given an opportunity, through the formal network, to voice their opinions, and to see that their experience is valued and that they can influence policy-making and its successful implementation. Everyone involved, whatever their position in an agency's heirarchy, can appreciate the significance of their role and their potential influence on other parts of the system. For clients, their immediate, often rapidly changing, needs are met as well as their long-term needs. For policy-makers, the structure forges close links between policy-making, implementation and networking, thus improving their ability to identify and prioritize training needs, areas requiring further research and development, gaps in provision and areas currently overresourced. The last is especially important given the natural reluctance of agencies to redistribute resources once allocated.

Balancing upstream and downstream work

A key function of the structure is to enable a balance to be held between upstream and downstream work.

'Downstream' case management: the inter-agency team or panel

The inter-agency panel set up with Elmore II support was intended to give participants first-hand experience of what might be achieved by structured coordination. The immediate objective was to coordinate the case management of young people identified by agencies or individual schools as having fallen 'through the net'. This was a departure from the more familiar multi-professional assessment of children with special educational needs, in that the only qualification required was evidence that a young person had fallen, or was at risk of falling, 'through the net'. Independent assessors gathered information, in person, and used this as the basis for a high-quality report. Taking one person, the assessor, to the informants rather than the more usual practice of gathering the information on paper and by post was more expensive but produced a more useful report, and brought other benefits.

For its members, the inter-agency panel demonstrated a different model of case management. The traditional approach was for the agency making the initial expression of concern to call a case conference. This might include members of other agencies (though more commonly it was an intra-agency meeting), and led to subsequent case conferences within each contributing agency that might then each conduct its own review independently of the others. For the majority this strategy works reasonably well. A young person with a statement of special educational needs will, for example, have a key worker, usually based close to them in a school. Children and young people 'through the net' are in a very different situation. The central problem may be, first, to find them and, second, to find someone they are prepared to talk to, who may, as Elmore II's panel demonstrated, be 'unusual', i.e. not an agency employee and not a professional. The panel therefore plays a crucial role in supporting the key worker. Having taken a referral and appointed an independent assessor, the panel discusses the assessor's report at its next meeting and appoints a key worker. Key workers undertake this role with permission to be creative, knowing who to turn to for support and advice and when to report back to the panel with further ideas, negotiated with the young person, about a suitable package of support. Depending on their agency status and experience, key workers may also double as case managers. Key workers from the voluntary sector would normally require a case manager based in one of the agencies or in the inter-agency team/panel.

Several objectives are met in this model. The child's needs are put first. A management plan and appropriate resources are put together by the person most likely to make and retain personal contact with the young person and to consider his/her wishes and feelings. The key worker is likely to be someone already known to the young person, possibly a youth worker, teacher or someone from the voluntary sector. Current work in 'kinship care' (Broad *et al.* 2001) is an exciting recent extension of the use of what Elmore II referred to as 'interesting' and effective key workers. Elmore III was also experimenting with the use of older teenagers as mentors for vulnerable young people, supporting, and supported by, key workers and case managers. Strategies such as these mean that a case which seems impossible becomes more manageable. Other practitioners then feel encouraged and become more willing to work with difficult cases in the future. This would, in Huxham's (1996: 241) terms, exemplify 'collaborative advantage', since agencies have achieved together 'something unusually creative . . . that no organization could have produced on its own'. But this way of working does not (and this is very important) undermine the work of any agency or practitioner already involved with the client.

There are other benefits. Practitioners from different agencies are brought together with a job they have all agreed, and have given up time to do, in a spirit of mutual tolerance and trust. Panel members can express their opinions freely and learn about others' viewpoints, prejudices and fears. Panel meetings offer a relatively safe place where ideas contributing to good practice can be discussed, with opportunities to challenge others' philosophies, concepts and language, and be challenged in return.

A significant element in the appeal to practitioners of Elmore II's panel was that it allowed them a degree of independence from mainstream agency attitudes and behaviours without compromising their professional standards. Here was an opportunity to meet on neutral territory, with permission to work with young people in ways they considered professionally appropriate, but which would have seemed subversive within the confines of normal agency business. The pressure to conform was removed. They were not asked to make judgements about whether time spent on one young person might have been better spent on preventative work elsewhere. No agency colleagues reproached them or ridiculed their efforts. This renewed professional confidence and motivation. Agencies and practitioners were as likely, it seemed, to become victims of 'learned helplessness' as their clients. Paradoxically, involvement with an inter-agency initiative appeared to increase, rather than reduce, the value of the specialist expertise of professionals. They felt fully capable, in short, of 'doing the right thing, at the right time, for the right reasons'. This was welcomed at a time when morale was low and the sense of agency and professional purpose blunted. For many practitioners in primary care agencies during the early and mid-1990s political interference and a lack of funding had distorted agency purpose.

Because of the panel's focus on 'through the netness', panel members gained a clearer picture of the pressures on young people in the locality and of their own responses to these pressures than they would otherwise have had. This was especially true for teachers and headteachers and generated ideas for training and for future research and preventative work based on a realistic understanding of community needs. In this situation, it was easier to engage with an ecological perspective in a manner that was practicable locally.

Cost highlighted more than any other factor the need for meta-strategy and legislation. The evidence from other sources is unequivocal on this point, whether from the costs of Care in the Community or from business management. Huxham's (1996) experience, for example, suggested that successful collaboration was expensive but that cost should be seen in the context of the advantage gained from the collaboration. For legislators, evidence in the literature on school exclusion suggests that making agencies pay for the 'true' costs of failure to take responsibility for clients who fall 'through the net' can be an effective strategy to improve services. Charging schools for young people they fail to educate encourages them to review their provision to include these children and, in the event of any reluctance to change, enables LEAs to insist that funding follows the pupil. The inter-agency panel operated at a time when these issues were becoming better understood. The implementation of the 1989 Children Act and initial steps towards the development of local authority children's services plans followed closely on the introduction to schools of LMS. Until distorted by loss of funding, agency purpose could be reaffirmed to include those at the margins. There was still, however, the tendency to argue too simplistically, in support of inter-agency work, that it would cost less. Agencies were not then bearing the cost, financially, of young people 'through the net', and could not see how working with them would do other than increase their costs. The cost to professional morale and the waste of young people's opportunities seemed less important set against a deficit bank balance.

Inter-agency support teams or panels of this kind can expect some measure of success and are likely to be positively evaluated, not only for the quality of their downstream work but in terms of improved inter-professional relationships and changed attitudes. Practitioners and clients both benefit, and although the young people selected for assessment and case management are among the most difficult known to the agencies, they can be 'pulled back into the system'. Key workers are able to put together 'exciting packages', reminiscent of Intermediate Treatment working methods in the 1970s. Structures of this kind act as a catalyst and useful practices are carried forward and integrated into normal agency practice. In the case of Elmore II, the experience of the panel had encouraged members to extend their idea of what they thought they could achieve, and this indirectly extended the remit of their agency. Agency boundaries, they found, were more elastic than they had previously thought.

'Upstream' preventative work: The Network

The word 'network' is deceptively simple and suffers from heavy use in an ever extending range of contexts. 'The Network' featured prominently in the development of Elmore I and was introduced early in the life of Elmore II. In some respects, it was the most innovative, and enduring, aspect of Elmore II, as a resource for practitioners working with children and young people. The reasons for this can be inferred from its activities and approach (see

Chapter 4). Its unusual combination of informal formality and powerful influence made it a non-threatening meeting place for practitioners from any part of any agency hierarchy. At a time when the primary care agencies were becoming increasingly dependent on the voluntary sector for services and case management this was especially important. Many voluntary sector workers were employed on short-term part-time contracts. Some were new to the area and newly qualified, and the network provided support, encouragement and the opportunity to meet others working in the same field. Agendas were arranged in response to issues raised by participants and minutes were sent to all participants, whether or not they attended. In this way information was shared widely and everyone was included and could contribute. As a whole, formal networks of this kind provide a wide range of information and evidence to support change. Although they are self-managing, attendance does normally require authority from senior managers. If practitioners have, as they more commonly do now, a responsibility to incorporate inter-agency work as part of their job descriptions, that is not a problem, but until very recently, attendance could sometimes arouse suspicion among colleagues – even though most network meetings are organized to interfere as little as possible with the working day. Until senior managers, as systemic thinkers, see networks such as these as helpful to the system as a whole, networks are unlikely to flourish. This failure of joined up thinking continues to impede the progress of joined up action.

Viewed systemically, therefore, formal networks are significant. According to Campbell *et al.* (1989: 12):

> The single most important intervention to enable organizations to manage change productively is to increase awareness of the way feedback is passed through the organization. Feedback is the life blood of any system. In order to work together, people at both the top and bottom of a hierarchical organization must have feedback about their behaviour from other levels of the hierarchy, and in order for a system to remain viable within its environment, feedback must be passed back and forth between the internal organization and the external environment.

Campbell *et al.* (1994: 15), developing this theme, consider that 'Complex human systems exist for a purpose, and the purpose creates a context that in turn gives meaning to all of the activity that takes place in that context.' In the context of this study, the coordinating structure creates channels through which feedback on this scale can pass. Without it, those who value feedback are deprived of it and opportunities for others to contribute are minimal. Feedback is reduced to the informal, passing between those who share the same beliefs and outlook and get on with each other at a personal level. This explains the value placed in Elmore I and II on their networks' capacity to 'formalize informal networks', and to provide the opportunity for members to challenge accepted agency and professional opinion. Since all members of any agency could attend, and the meetings were in every sense non-hierarchical, they also became a training ground for the development of inter-professional and inter-personal skills.

The significance of the network in a coordinating structure thus centres on its role in the feedback loop. Unless all those involved with the client group can be involved, important information and insights are lost. Individual cases are never, for reasons of confidentiality, discussed at network meetings, but the issues arising from casework are. This is particularly relevant in the case of TTN children and young people. Since agency practitioners rarely, by definition, case manage those who fall 'through the net', they are unable to provide feedback about these young people's situation to their senior managers. Nor are they able to share experience of the successful inter-agency case management of such children. Thus the only feedback circulating is informal and negative, a story of professional and agency incapacity and failure. In the coordinating model suggested here, the support team/panel provides, through effective inter-agency case management, the matter for positive feedback and the opportunity to change beliefs and behaviour. These positive changes in attitude arising out of successful practice can then be disseminated throughout the whole system via the network.

However, this virtuous circle is incomplete, as Elmore II demonstrated, without the existence of a meta-strategy designed by policy-makers, taking account of the feedback received from other parts of the system. In the projects outlined in Chapter 5, the recognition that feedback mattered was a strong feature, but there seemed to be no formal structures through which it could pass. Everyone has their own personal informal network of friends, family and colleagues, structured by, for example, national and religious festivals, and events in family and working life. We take this so much for granted that we do not bother to analyse how this is achieved, though we are well aware of what happens when communication structures and/or processes break down. In the inter-agency arena, with TTN children and young people, when no one can be sure quite what will work best, and creative solutions are required, everyone depends on effective communication, structured in such a way as to encourage and value everyone's contribution.

Mort (1999: 234), in a description of The Network (Elmore I), makes it sound remarkably like family life:

> The most significant feature of the Network is the commitment which its members display ... to the work of their own agencies and in general to the Network itself ... Not all agencies are necessarily represented regularly at the monthly meeting ... yet people frequently turn up saying something like 'I haven't been for two or three years for a variety of reasons but I intend to come regularly from now on, I think it is really important.' For such a nebulous, formless body, this commitment is remarkable, Perhaps it is a kind of corporate manifestation of the team loyalty and mutual support which enables individual projects to function.

A vehicle for collaboration 'fit for the purpose'

It will be clear from the foregoing that although the panel/team is primarily concerned with downstream case management, and the network with upstream preventative work, the distinction is by no means watertight: it is the same river. What matters is that both are integrated in the same overall communication structure within which the voices of all those involved with the client group can be heard.

For some, the model described here will seem unduly prescriptive. Hambleton *et al.* (1995: 75), in their study of the collaborative council, suggest in relation to 'getting the right model' that:

There is a whole range of collaborative activities: some of which have been clearly thought out at the beginning and others which have grown in an organic way. It is important that the vehicle of collaboration is fit for the purpose intended. This will require budgets, objectives, roles, structures and process to be clearly defined; occasionally it will require joint arrangements to be time limited. All of this will require clear definition and clarity of purpose.

In this case a model 'fit for the purpose' had to meet the needs of any client group at risk of falling 'through the net'. Proof of 'fitness' also came to mean that the model should be capable of being transferred from one locality to another, achieved in Elmore III (see p. 90), and that it should integrate upstream and downstream work. Wilson and Charlton (1997: 16–17) suggest that an effective model: 'is not meant to be prescriptive . . . [it] describes a composite picture drawn from experience . . . the purpose of the model is to provide a framework for examining critical success factors that impinge upon the partnership management process.'

The model outlined here was developed because without it agency difficulties could not be resolved and children's needs would continue to be met in a manner which was unreliable, wasteful of energy and damaging to everyone. The test of a successful model was that it should work for those who challenged the agencies most. The tripartite pattern of the model separates the qualitatively different, though interconnected, activities of policy and planning, implementation and networking. The structure protects each from the constraints and modes of operation of the others, but at the same time creates communication lines between them. Inter-agency activity appropriate to each level can then be coordinated and communicated quickly, with outcomes monitored and evaluated. The measure of the structure's success is that it helps agencies to retain children within their local support network and restore to it those that fall through. A model 'fit for the purpose' in terms of inter-agency coordination is characterized primarily, therefore, by its ability to integrate prevention and cure, upstream and downstream.

Conclusion

One of the reasons for success may be the conception of 'through the net' in a way which refuses to compartmentalize children. Most coordinating models for children at risk are designed for certain subgroups of the wider category of children at risk which, from the evidence of the literature and

Box 7.2 Case history 2

Elaine (aged 15 at the time of interview)

When she is 13 Elaine is referred to social services by the police, as she has violently assaulted her mother. Her mother is taken to hospital. Her ESW is involved, and states that her attendance at school is good. It is discovered that Elaine is angry with her mother because she has been told that her father, who left before she was born, is not who she has been told he is. The ESW assessment states that the main issues Elaine has to confront are her anger at her mother and her own self-image. The ESW closes the case. However, five days later Elaine is not in school and the school is worried about the mother's safety, as she has returned home. The ESW continues to visit the home but the case is not allocated to a social worker. The ESW states that Elaine is emotionally disturbed and decides not to visit the home again because this may provoke Elaine to make another attack on her mother. Elaine is allotted a social worker two months after the initial attack on her mother. Meanwhile, the ESW has contacted the psychiatric unit and they make an assessment. Elaine is placed with them.

> Things at home got bad when I was ten or eleven. I still went to school and no one knew. I skived the last couple of months at middle school . . . Then I went to upper school but I never started. The ESW came to see me then my mum contacted Social Services who told the police. I was at the psychiatric unit for six months. It was more relaxed. (Elaine)

Elaine is put on an interim care order. The psychiatric unit take over coordinating the inter-agency meetings and update others on the treatment Elaine is receiving. Elaine does not want to return home, but social services express concern about care staff being able to facilitate appropriate care arrangements for her, considering her volatile nature. A plan to integrate Elaine into secondary school with support from the psychiatric unit is discussed and agreed. However, the plan cannot go ahead as the school is full. The review meeting is informed. The psychiatric unit staffs begin to liaise with another school and it is agreed that there should be no more formal meetings regarding integration.

Elaine is accommodated by social services in a residential home and begins to attend school. The case is closed by the ESW. However, she is re-referred to the ESW one month later as she has only attended school for ten out of thirty days. The ESW contacts the social worker for information. Elaine is now being accommodated at another residential home, and may be moved again. Elaine is depressed and not attending school. Social services are trying to find an out-of-county placement for her. Social services would like Elaine to go to the off-site tutorial unit and the school agrees. At the age of 15 Elaine starts at the tutorial unit and the ESW closes the case. The social worker feels that the burden of intervention has been with social services and that the boundaries of where work begins and ends are unclear. The social worker commented that until things get serious, and 'they slip through the net', these young people feel there is no one to turn to. When I interviewed Elaine she did not want to talk in detail about what had happened with her mother. She said they were getting on better if they 'kept off serious things. It doesn't help talking, I want something sorted out.' She stays in residential care and is placed in a flat when she reaches 16: 'I wish I'd not missed so much normal school. I'd like to go to college.'

(After Lloyd 1994)

Box 7.3 Case history with inter-agency intervention

John (aged 15 at the time of interview)

According to John's mother, it was difficult for her to get help at the beginning:

> When he was six he was caught nicking sweets. I called the police to give him a warning. Sweets to skateboard to bikes to burglaries. Every time I was telling the police: 'Please do something with this kid before it gets bigger', and every time it got bigger I said the same thing. I've called the shots. (Mother)

John could have been referred early to an inter-agency youth support team/panel (YST) by his mother, the ESW or the school.

John was first referred to the ESW service when he was aged 11. The ESW notes state that 'mother appears not able to cope', and it is suggested that she contacts the children's psychiatric services. At this point the psychiatric social worker (PSW) agreed to take the case and works with the family for ten weeks.

The PSW's ten-week input might have been more effective had it not taken place in isolation and had it been supported by a YST key worker.

There is a second referral to the ESW service from the school because of his 'continued absence from school'. The ESW tries to move him from the school, but two schools refuse him a place. He is then permanently excluded from his current school. The ESW tries to involve social services, who state that the main problem is education and close the case.

> I think the problem was that he would be so far behind with his schooling that, if he actually had to go into a class, it was so embarrassing for him, so the best thing to do was either play up so

that he got kicked out or not go at all. Which is a shame. So he left school a year before he should have. He doesn't read or write and with his offences he will find it hard to get a job. (Mother)

The ESW recognized the need for social services involvement, e.g. to offer the family support or counselling, but did not have the appropriate authority to ensure that social services make a contribution to the support plan.

John is not at school and is in trouble with the police. His mother states that the family are in crisis and need social services' help. He continues to be in trouble with the police on a weekly basis and is in court nearly every week with additional offences. The court cases are continually adjourned to consider these. These offences have now become more serious and include burglary and stealing cars.

During the time the ESW worked with the school to find John a place, the YST worker could have had ongoing contact with John out of school and been looking at the wider issues of motivation, family relationships and his criminal activities. The YST worker could invoke the networking process involving a wider range of relevant agencies, e.g. youth service, further education opportunities, skills training, careers.

John is now 15, and at an education case conference it is proposed that he attend an off-site education provision. The ESW's intervention ceases. His mother contacts social services stating she cannot cope. John is taken into care. He spends a year in a children's home, during which time he is moved from the Social Services Adolescent Team to the Juvenile Justice Team and remanded into care as part of a remand placement order. He fails to conform to this order and a secure order is requested by social services. John is later detained in a young offenders institute.

In cases such as this the YST worker would provide long-term continuity and coordination for the young person and their family. This might have eliminated the need for John to be received into care. As a minimum, the YST worker would have ensured that the question of his education would be pursued once he was in a residential home, and ensured continuity of attention for him and his family.

(After Lloyd 1994)

It is not by any means clear how personal advisers are to be supported, where they would go for help and how long it would take to arrange it. Current work with personal advisers in Sunderland (Marshall and Elliott 2001) suggests that this is indeed a problem and that inter-agency support networks are being considered as part of the solution.

Box 7.3 demonstrates how inter-agency approaches can help to prevent some of the problems escalating and how agencies can be encouraged to coordinate their services through the use of an independent inter-agency body. Initiatives such as Sure Start and Connexions make a successful outcome more likely than previously but sustained support over a number of years for individual young people remains an issue, particularly at the critical points of change and transition. These were the points Elmore III addressed through the employment a family–school–community links worker. Without the support of teams such as Elmore I's ECST, inter-agency practitioners still risk being left to manage on their own in situations only manageable with the long-term support of others.

Part of the answer lies in the new approaches to case management which develop when practitioners begin working across agency boundaries, or indeed within them, with those who could potentially fall 'through the net'. Many of these are to be found developing in pupil referral units, behaviour support teams and integrated support services (Barrow 1998; Glenny 2001) and in the work of national charities (Include 1998). In the traditional approach, outlined above, support continued to come from individual agencies, or possibly only one of them, so that problems were rarely resolved. There was little chance to prepare beforehand, to gather information and to marshall possible resources, and plenty of opportunity for mutual recrimination. Even when agencies agreed to hold joint case conferences, problems with diaries, travelling time and expense prevented them from being fully attended. The case management model, which has been developing as agencies become more accustomed to working across boundaries, demonstrates the difference in outcome when an independent assessor gathers, collates and shares the information beforehand, rather than expecting individual practitioners to arrive at the meeting with information which others may not have had time to consider.

There is still much to learn, and to make more explicit, about what is needed to support the detailed and careful case management of individuals on the margins, and about how to create a system allowing this kind of care to become part of universal provision. To explore the difficulty posed by 'critical points' more closely, the next section outlines a case history in which local inter-agency cooperation had been a significant feature for several years but had been, despite that, unable to prevent a tragedy.

'Difficult to place' adults: the Report of the Inquiry into the circumstances leading to the death of Jonathan Newby

Inquiries into the death of, for example, care workers by mentally disturbed adults, or of abused children, are of special relevance as a reminder that it is problems that fall 'through the net' rather than people, and that we learn much about how to solve these problems when faced with some of their more extreme consequences. The Newby Inquiry is significant since it concerns a client of the ECST, who was therefore surrounded by more support than might otherwise have been the case. This team was widely regarded as an example of good inter-agency practice, in a city in which practitioners had over many years attempted to establish an inter-agency system to cater for individuals at risk or who might pose risk to others. The Inquiry could, therefore, be expected to shed light on what further problems were still unsolved and what implications there might be for future inter-agency policy and practice.

This example concerns a young volunteer, Jonathan Newby, who worked in a hostel run by a local charity. In 1993 he was killed by a resident, John Rous, a middle-aged man who suffered from schizophrenia with a 'concomit-ant severe disorder of personality' (Oxfordshire Health Authority 1995: 3). Under the terms of a National Health Service Executive circular (HSG (94) 27), 'In cases of homicide, it will always be necessary to hold an inquiry which is independent of the providers involved' (p. 3). In this case, the Com-mittee of Inquiry had a lengthy task, since 'John Rous had been in the care of practically every statutory and voluntary organisation in Oxford and else-where . . . Sixty witnesses were invited to give evidence . . . Fifty-four written statements were received, forty-five people gave oral evidence' (p. 5).

John Rous had a childhood resembling those of our previous case studies in some respects. It was a childhood which would almost certainly come to the attention of the Early Years initiatives developing today, and of those assessing the needs of children and their families (DoH 1998b; DoH, DfEE and Home Office 2000). He never knew his natural father, was abandoned by his mother at the age of three and thereafter was cared for by foster parents. He left school at 15 and travelled around the country from job to job, during which time he began to abuse drugs. At some time in his twenties a person-ality disorder was diagnosed, followed by a diagnosis of schizophrenia. Then followed a period of placements in rehabilitation units, halfway houses, and lodgings in the community, coupled with attendance as a day patient in hospital. There was a six-month period of imprisonment, followed by accommodation in a hostel, once more in the community. During this time there were two occasions on which he had physically assaulted hospital staff. He continued to receive medical attention as an outpatient and maintained links with his probation officer. Although there were concerns about his erratic attendance as an outpatient, his psychosis was deemed to be under control. For the five years prior to the murder he had been a client of the ECST, during which time there was a degree of stability. However, behaviour in his then place of residence deteriorated, there were concerns once more about his drinking and he was believed to be depressed and suicidal on occasion. The ECST workers continued their efforts to find suitable accom-modation, which eventually resulted in a placement in the hostel in which Jonathan Newby was a volunteer. This was not a happy period for John. He wished to leave, was irritated by the rules and lack of money and was unable to make friends among a group of people very different from him in educa-tion and background. In 1993 he found a girlfriend, who became pregnant, John Rous believing himself to be the father.

Jonathan Newby, who had previously worked in a number of other hostels, also found this hostel a difficult place. He and the other volunteers all had concerns about safety there. During the summer of 1993, John's alcohol consumption rose and he became short of money, but no one noticed any deterioration in his mental state. Matters came to a head on 9 October. He pestered workers on duty for a loan, but there was a system for this which he had already exceeded and his request was refused. Later in the day, he asked Jonathan for money, adopting an intensely threatening manner. Jonathan, in sole charge of the hostel at the time, at first refused but later, under even more duress, gave him an IOU, whereupon John went to the local pub. At the Inquiry he said that it was there that he decided to kill someone, and of three possible people, decided on Jonathan Newby.

During the course of the Inquiry, the committee found that all the witnesses who knew him, 'be they friends, support workers, carers or doctors', were united in their 'astonishment and disbelief at the news that John Rous had committed an act of such violence as to result in a death . . . no witness . . . suggested that he or she had ever felt physically threatened.' On the evidence available, the Inquiry concluded that 'the killing of Jonathan Newby was an act of horrific violence, it was also an act wholly out of character for John Rous and of a nature unforeseen by all who knew him' (p. 31).

Implications for inter-agency work

The Inquiry highlighted, as many other similar inquiries have done, a range of issues relating to the pressures on those who work with 'difficult to place' people. The implications for inter-agency work are no less relevant for those working on behalf of 'through the net' children and young people. The Inquiry was in no doubt that: 'John Rous presented a severe challenge to those providing care. He was homeless, he had a severe and enduring mental illness and a concomitant severe disorder of the personality. The problem which John Rous presented is not uncommon' (p. 50).

Cases such as these suggest the need for more longitudinal studies and greater continuity of provision across age groups and over time. The evidence provided in Elmore II's interviews with young people over the age of 16 provide some of the missing data between the inter-agency provision surrounding children and that surrounding adults – Connexions (DfES 2001a), one of the first initiatives to bridge this gap, is rightly named. It is significant, for example, that independent estimates of the numbers of TTN young people, in a city such as Oxford, produced very similar results to adults in the same city considered to be DTP, and, equally significantly, the older age groups were more strongly associated with mental health problems. Other studies suggest that mental health problems in children and young people have been underestimated (Kurtz et al. 1994).

In this case, witnesses described a long history of poor relationships between health and social services: 'There always seemed to be financial constraints on both authorities that appeared to shift the focus of planning more to what we could pass on to whom rather than how we can build services jointly' (Oxfordshire Health Authority 1995: 55). The Inquiry commented that in these circumstances it was hardly surprising that voluntary agencies took on the role of providing accommodation and care for the mentally ill. Thus neglect of some of society's most vulnerable people had led to the voluntary sector filling gaps in public sector provision. The report heavily criticized poor management, monitoring and evaluation in the public sector, commenting that in these circumstances it was hardly surprising that voluntary agencies took on the role of providing accommodation and care for the mentally ill. These difficulties meant that the Care Programme Approach had been slow to develop locally and had only been fully implemented in 1994, whereas it could have been in place three years earlier. Similar comments could be said to apply in the slow response in England and Wales to the implementation of the 1989 Children Act.

Issues for practitioners

For practitioners, maintaining up-to-date personal knowledge of their clients is a major problem. In the Newby case, important events in John Rous's life in the days immediately before the tragedy were not known either to the workers and inmates of the hostel or to key workers. But in the evidence presented to the Inquiry, one of his street friends gave a different account of events in the days preceding 9 October from that given by John himself or his fellow hostel inmates. He had apparently told this friend how much he disliked being at the hostel, how disturbed he was by one of the other inmates and that he wanted to be put in hospital in a lock-up ward. The need for close supervision and the importance of community and other networks bring one back to the school context and the importance of initiatives such as buddy systems, peer counselling and school-based self-referral systems to school counsellors, school nurses and mentors. Much too, can clearly be achieved through initiatives such as the Quality Protects Programme and the Healthy Schools Programme (DoH 1998a; DoH/DfEE and Home Office 2000).

Coping with a crisis

In the immediate crisis, Jonathan Newby recorded in John Rous's notes that on being refused an IOU by him, John Rous had become extremely threatening. 'He called 999 and told the police he was going to kill me. He went into his room to get a knife so I locked myself into the office and he proceeded to attempt to kick the door in' (Oxfordshire Health Authority 1995: 42). Jonathan Newby records that he gave him an IOU at this point, whereupon John Rous left saying he would go to the night shelter. In fact, he went to the pub, from where, it transpired, he made a 999 call to the police. It was later established that he had used a pay phone, warning the police, in a conversation of just on two minutes, that he intended to kill someone at the hostel, and how and why. The operator took no action and within 40 minutes Jonathan Newby was dead – the result of a tragic failure 'to do the right thing, at the right time, for the right reasons'. It is a failure to which practitioners will all too readily relate, in terms of warning signs not heeded, or missed, of false alarms raised too often, and of inexperience. Chance may have a part to play, though not generally at more than one or two points in the chain of causation, but effective structures and processes can at least reduce the risks.

Joining up the action

Although only a few of the recommendations of the Newby Inquiry are touched on here, their concerns focus on the same issues relating to legislation, strategic and operational matters, professional practice and financial arrangements noted elsewhere in this study. The Inquiry recognized that Oxford had an unusually high number of homeless people, among them an increasing number of people with mental illnesses with fewer than average statutory services for them. This meant that there was a greater burden on the voluntary sector. The Inquiry considered that 'a national programme is required to tackle this problem' and that 'health authorities, social services departments and housing authorities should establish a specialist outreach and care team for homeless people with severe mental illness' (Oxfordshire Health Authority 1995: 52). In effect these recommendations address a difficulty experienced in relation to a specific group – a good outcome in terms of securing provision for that group from statutory agencies but not one which addresses the underlying problem of how the system as a whole could channel feedback and information more productively. Feedback, as one might expect of a commodity described as the 'life blood' of systems and institutions, drains 'through the net' as quickly as the clients.

Structure and process issues were thus reflected in the factors which the Inquiry believed had resulted in an accident 'black spot', interlocked in what the Inquiry described as 'a chain of causation' (p. 140). As with the 'critical points' noted in agency relationships with young people, the Inquiry identified the occasions upon which the chain of events leading to Jonathan Newby's death could have been broken. These likewise centred on details which can be routed back to the interplay of upstream and downstream work. Issues raised had implications for each level of inter-agency cooperation. Thus closer liaison among front-line workers, more attention to detail in terms of record keeping, monitoring and supervision for key workers and middle managers, and the provision of appropriate training and supervision for inter-agency practitioners all featured. Most heavily criticized was the lack of cooperation between senior managers and policy-makers in health and social services.

What was missing for this group was inter-agency cooperation at policy-making level. This, it will be recalled, contrasts with the situation in Lothian, where it had been strategists from the two lead agencies for young people that had promoted the principles which eventually drove the policy for cooperation forward, despite initial opposition. In the Newby case, the void created by lack of commitment and support from the top for the section of the population who, by any standards, were most at risk of falling through the net was filled by voluntary organizations, many of whom were least well prepared for this. The effects of the lack of strategy can be detected in all 16 of the Committee of Inquiry's 'critical points' in the 'chain of causation'. An example concerns training. One of the self-appointed tasks of the Network, itself a product of the voluntary sector, supported by individual agency practitioners (usually in their own time), was to organize training for those working across agency boundaries. Without inter-agency strategy, this could not be expected to satisfy demand or provide a structured service to suit the wide range of practitioners working with DTP people. Thus a young volunteer, like many others, received 'no appropriate training in working with people with chronic and enduring mental illness' (p. 141).

The Newby Inquiry, among many other similar studies relating to children (e.g. Sereny 1995), and the interviews with young people once again point to the way in which systems and process interact. These dimensions can be expressed very simply in terms of two intersecting axes (Figure 7.1). On a point scale of 0–10 on each axis, positive points indicate successful inter-agency practice and negative points indicate failure and the risk of falling 'through the net'. In any particular case it is possible, using the grid, to

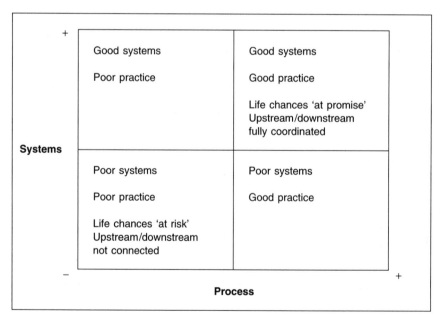

Figure 7.1 Interaction between systems and process

identify factors leading to inter-agency accident 'black spots' and occasions in the chain of causation where a tragedy could have been prevented. In the Newby case, despite the many good features of local inter-agency practice, lack of attention to monitoring and overall strategy had resulted in a chain of causation which brought the case as a whole into the left-hand bottom quadrant.

Tools for assessing risk or for highlighting areas of strength or weakness in the management of a case, or for evaluation and training, serve as a useful reminder of how system and process interact. Even more, such tools can suggest where further research, development and training to promote better practice in and between agencies is required. Inter-agency cooperation has the potential to improve practice, but only when coordinated in a well maintained system integrating structure and process, prevention and crisis management. Enriching feedback and improving its circulation is what matters most in creating a 'learning system' (Senge 1999), and we can expect to learn as much from success as failure – for every John Rous, there is a Nobel Prize winner. The success of programmes such as 'Seven Up' suggests that the general public greatly values feedback, but our systems for improving its amount and quality are more limited than they need be, and the channels of information across time as well as across agency boundaries are easily blocked. Even in a school, for example, among students leaving at 16, false assumptions may be made about them which subsequent knowledge would, if available, dispel: the student who left under a cloud, but got in touch later having done very well; the Asian girl who left school at 16, assumed by the school to have married but in fact headed for further, and eventually higher, education. There are also the students for whom the school pulled out all the stops in terms of innovative packages of support and who, against all the odds, went on to lead full and happy lives. So much of that feedback is lost. This study has been concerned with 'through the netness' not simply because of the plight of some of those who fall through but because of what can be learnt about how to build a structure which will make the most of the commitment and creativity of all its participants.

Developing and maintaining a communication structure: roles and responsibilities

A sustainable structure, however simple, requires maintenance. The roles referred to in this study are principally concerned with that, and have been developed over the years by front-line workers within the familiar structures of an agency. The difficulty for practitioners out in the rough between the agencies in the early days of inter-agency cooperation was that so often there was no structure within which to work and front-line workers depended almost entirely on the inter-agency team itself for mutual support. Despite their best efforts, feedback stayed locked within the team. The projects drawn on earlier all recognized the importance of feedback but there was no circulation system and no structure to support it – what Senge (1999) calls a 'learning infrastructure'.

Hand in hand with the development of new roles has been the development of new terms to describe familiar roles, reinterpreted in response to the challenge of joined up action. Among inter- and intra-agency workers most aspects of these roles are interchangeable. Everyone will be involved to a greater or lesser extent as networkers. Independent assessors and network minders, on the other hand, also need, on the evidence of all three Elmore projects, high levels of inter-professional skills. For all individuals holding these roles the same pattern of planning, action and networking emerging between agencies was repeated within agencies and, again, within their own work. Thus each inter-agency worker engages with the tension between upstream and downstream, between planning, thinking and networking. For individuals, these dilemmas are argued out in the form of an internal dialogue, as vigorously as they are in discussions with colleagues or within the network.

That familiar roles should develop in new ways, and new roles emerge, is an important feature of work with marginalized people across agency boundaries. Among them is the developing role of the para-professional, of which the family–school–community links worker in Elmore III provides a good example, and for whom it was said that 'no boundary seemed to exist' (p. 91). Although this ease belies its position in a carefully constructed support and communication system, the role is rooted in the local community and fulfilled by someone closer to the most marginalized members of that community than most professionals can ever be. Writers in development studies, such as Chambers (1997: 183), would not be surprised: 'professionals . . . have had such different criteria and preferences from local people. Their life experiences, working environments, values, reward systems, livelihood strategies and personal interests all differ. Without major reversals, there is no way they could share the same realities'. Although many of Chambers's examples come from India and Africa, they are no less relevant to the UK. The strength of a community network is in the voices that can be heard there. 'In the amorphous, loose knit environment of the Network there are few structural constraints. There is plenty of space for entrepreneurial potential' (Mort 1999: 234). As the basic building block in a well maintained inter-agency structure this potential can be realized.

Key workers

Among front-line workers, the term key worker is very familiar and long established. In education, the Warnock Report (1978) introduced the concept in its recommendation that a 'named person' be designated as an advocate for parents of children under five, for parents of schoolchildren and 'at the moment of leaving school for young people, particularly those with more severe and complex disabilities, [who] may find themselves receiving far less support than at any time before . . . to whom they may turn for advice on which service or which professional to approach for help' (para. 10.92).

Thus key workers are associated with situations in which the client is the concern of more than one agency, and where there is degree of volatility or uncertainty about future placements or care. Looking back (see Chapter 2), we can see that this role has developed wherever there is a coordinating structure, as we saw in, for example, the Scottish Children's Hearing, multi-professional assessment and the Working Together Protocols for Children on 'at risk' registers. Key workers have been central in the probation service and in social services, for children looked after and, as we have seen, for adults with mental health or other problems requiring multi- or inter-agency support. Herbert (1998: 107) describes the role, in relation to pre-school children, in this way: 'When families work with a wide range of professionals they may develop a close relationship with one of them and this person should be seen as the "key" worker for that family, taking the role of co-ordinator and facilitator.'

The term has spread rapidly in schools, especially since the introduction of the (now revised) Code of Practice (DfE 1994b; DfES 2001c), in response to the move towards inclusion. As in society at large, situations in school are more flexible than they were, and are set to become more so, with an increased range of professionals based there. Key workers in schools are required to keep track of their charges, and to act as advocates and intermediaries and as someone to turn to for help in setting and achieving educational targets.

Network minders

Where key workers hold the ring for individual children and young people, network minders hold the ring for the inter-agency networks. This term, coined by Glenny (2000) in her evaluation of Elmore III, has been adopted here, in preference to 'coordinator', because it reflects the more fluid, empowering coordination role appropriate for the networks developing to support joined up action. Coordination, according to a dictionary definition, means 'bringing parts into proper relation', and a coordinator is 'one who adjusts, settles, fixes, organizes'. Although this is a good description of the nature of the role, especially in its implicit assumption of well developed interpersonal skills, a new term is needed for this new context. For Glenny (2000: 8), 'The system needs a minder, not perhaps the normal notion of a leader, but somebody who can stand back from the web of roles and relationships that make up the Network and identify what is needed to ensure optimum functioning.'

The Elmore networks are characterized by open membership, much larger than the attendance at any one meeting would suggest, and network minders tend to 'emerge' rather than be formally appointed. Since running costs are low and the time commitment is light, there is not the same necessity to tie network minder appointments to anyone in any existing role. Indeed, to do so would be to undermine the essentially collegial, non-hierarchical nature of the network in which the appointment of the person with the most highly developed inter-professional skill is crucial: the person who can be relied on to 'do the right thing, at the right time, for the right reasons'. The network is a key element in an inter-agency communication structure and non-collegial behaviours in which participants hang on to status would quickly block the system and reduce the flow of feedback. Network minders ensure that meetings are chaired, that minutes are taken and circulated and that agendas respond to issues brought to the meeting. There may be some lightweight planning but there is plenty of space for the *ad hoc* raising of issues and for information exchange and the introduction of new members.

Originally, in Elmore I the network minder was a probation officer and the probation service covered the basic costs, mainly post and printing. In Elmore II the minder is currently a member of the education service with an inter-agency brief, but was previously minded by social services. In Elmore III, the network minder was an educational social worker, and the role has now passed to a school counsellor. The skills of the minder are focused on maintaining the inter-agency tenor of the network, its commitment to the client group and the development among its members of inter-agency under-standing. This can be achieved from something as simple sounding as an information exchange, or the introduction of practitioners new to the area. Glenny (2000: 7), watching this process as an evaluator, describes it thus:

> The key features of the information exchange were: raising awareness about individual roles and responsibilities; informing each other about the practice and policy issues that defined the priorities of each service; identifying similarities or differences in service operation that could facilitate or impede joint working.

The network minder is thus responsible for the quality of the feedback flowing through the system and the development of trust between network members. In Elmore III, for example, as trust grew over time, problems which had seemed at first insuperable gradually became manageable. Confidentiality, a major concern for Elmore III in its first year, had gone down the agenda as a serious problem two years later as network members gradually moved from problem- to solution-focused thinking. Finally, networkers themselves, Mort (1999: 232) found, 'are in one sense idealists. They want their clients treated as equal citizens and have high expectations of government and local authority . . . that the resources for what is needed should be supplied. They spend themselves unstintingly . . . and give the impression of caring deeply about their clients.'

Independent assessors

This role has been described in some detail in relation to Elmore II (see p. 75) and, again, it is a new interpretation of a familiar role, developed as part of the maintenance system promoting joined up action and requiring a high level of inter-personal and inter-professional skills. In the current proliferation of inter-agency agencies, such roles are emerging, with a range of titles: personal advisers, learning mentors, support workers and so on. Greater clarity is required to establish how each of these roles fits into the whole structure and what training and experience is required to fulfil the role. Without adequate training and support, their contribution is likely to be undervalued and ineffective.

Network brokers

Network-broking, a term developed by Elmore I in the mid-1980s to describe a key part of their inter-agency activity, was also adopted by Elmore II, and is beginning to be used more readily in this field. It is a role whose nature can be easily inferred from the way in which some tasks peculiar to the role are described. For example, key workers for children whose names have been placed on a Child Protection Register are described as having 'responsibility for completing the core assessment of the child and family *and securing contributions from core group members and others as necessary'* (DoH 2000: 5.13, emphasis added). A 'broker', according to a dictionary definition, is a 'middleman in bargains; agent, commissioner'. It is suggested here that network-broking is a key element in the role of coordinator, the means by which they 'bring parts into proper relation'. In schools, special educational needs coordinators (SENCOs) negotiate with colleagues to offer that them extra bit of ease and confidence which encourages them to expand their idea of what can be achieved – arranging, for example, to provide a specially trained learning support assistant to accompany a profoundly deaf child into a class where the teacher is unfamiliar with hearing impairment.

Steering groups

It would be easy to overlook the part played by steering groups in the development of the inter-agency projects described here. In the projects described in this study, steering groups took responsibility for monitoring and managing the day-to-day work of the projects in response to the gaps in provision identified by the local network. Unlike the networks, the steering groups are 'tight' rather than 'loose', with a small membership carefully selected to be representative of the agencies involved. Glenny (2000), in her evaluation of Elmore III, found that local headteachers and SENCOs considered the scene before the network was set up as 'sluggish and unresponsive so that a crisis had to be generated before any action would occur'. Headteachers and SENCOs had become:

> adept at moving around what they regarded as blockages in the system in order to achieve the support they needed. They viewed the development of the Network as beginning the process of making the system more coherent and effective for users. By examining the whole system of support its operation was made visible and channels of communication could be explicitly mapped and their functionality explored. The

Network had provided a forum for developing the fluidity of the system ... greatly enhanced by the energy and strategic action of the steering group ... [which] effectively provided the brain for the system, allowing it to reflect upon itself and change itself to be more responsive to users' needs.

(Glenny 2000: 7)

Was this, one wonders, what Warnock hoped for from Joint Consultative Committees? If so, ensuring that such groups maintain their energy and ability to 'think' is a vital part of how the coordinating structure as a whole is maintained and sustained. The network provided the 'ground', as it were, the part of the structure most likely to introduce new ideas and identify gaps in provision. The steering group acted on these ideas and managed the outcome in projects which were fed back through the system to policy-makers. 'Filling gaps' and removing 'blockages in the system' appear to be what galvanize practitioners into action, and nothing frustrates them more than distance from policy-makers.

Building bridges or demolishing barriers?

The role of network broker brings together much that has always gone on within and between agencies. It is a role carried out, for example, by pressure groups and other advocates for particular purposes or passions in almost any discipline. Here the role is formalized and made explicit. That it has become so is important in the context of joined up action, since it allows us to become more explicit about a question underlying the whole concept. To what extent do inter-agency practitioners build bridges or demolish barriers? Who decides in any particular instance? Pat Goodwin, Elmore I's first network minder, had reason to explore the connection between partnership, professionalism and coordination in some detail:

Being a partner means being someone who has a share or a part with another or other persons, a partaker or a sharer in any form of enjoyment or possession. The word 'partner' has been used for centuries though its medieval form derives from the original Latin 'partitio' (partition) and this divisive meaning has remained at its centre. In its many social, political and scientific uses it has since developed as an all purpose term meaning everything from splitting apart to getting together. It should be used with care and only after those using it have discussed the question and decided what they wish to make clear (or maybe conceal).

(In OCVA 1991: 39)

The tension in the word partnership is full of meaning for those anxious about threats to, or limitations that might be put on, their professionalism. Comments from the professionals interviewed in connection with Elmore II showed that this was a real concern for those embarking on inter-agency activity and networking. They were aware as professionals that they wanted 'to keep their patches safe'. They did not 'want to be rigid, but cannot do everything and need to accept their own and other people's limitations ... there needs to be some acceptance that boundaries exist' (OCVA 1991: *passim*).

How, in other words, can a professional – that is, one who has 'a vocation, a calling' (*Concise Oxford Dictionary*), whose inspiration, experience and motivation come from pursuing a profession, and developing the highest possible specialist expertise – be encouraged to work with, and understand, others not of the same calling? To what extent is it possible to promote the idea that it may be part of professionalism to be able to share it? How can professionals be encouraged to expand the boundaries of what they believe themselves capable of doing? These difficult issues are, and have been for years, addressed through network-broking, even though the role has not been made sufficiently explicit either within inter-agency structures or in the role of coordinator.

Conclusion

This chapter has moved from cases studies of TTN/DTP individuals to a discussion of the roles and responsibilities of those seeking to address 'through the net' agency problems. It has been noted above that an effective inter-agency structure depends on the same structure being mirrored within agencies and their institutions. An unfortunate, but unfortunately apt, alternative dictionary definition for a broker is a 'dealer in second-hand goods'. The history of marginalized people everywhere might seem to have been just that, in terms of lack of respect, opportunity and inequity. And some of our interview material makes this cruelly obvious: 'we were just going backwards and forwards from one to the other.' The same could be said more generally of 'wicked issues', each of which appears to require the same attention to the building of lightweight flexible structures encouraging the free flow of feedback and creative ideas from those on the ground with first-hand experience of the 'issue' in question. In terms of 'through the net' children, this first-hand experience is rooted in case work within existing agencies. The next chapter considers intra-agency structures designed to prevent children and young people falling through their first safety net outside the family.

CHAPTER EIGHT

Intra-agency teams:
special educational needs

Intra-agency structure

Two insights drew attention to coordinating structures within agencies. First, effective structures to coordinate upstream and downstream work within agencies appeared to be the first line of defence preventing individuals from falling 'through the net'. Second, a superficial comparison between an inter-agency team for 'difficult to place' adults and an intra-agency team such as an LEA's special educational needs support services, or a school special educational needs team, suggested structural and process similarities between them.

The link in the Elmore model between a team and a network and the use of terms such as network-broking were also relevant in the school context and as part of the developing role of the SENCO. However, by comparison with the inter-agency model outlined in Chapter 6, the third element, the network, is as easily overlooked within agencies as it is between them. It is not that networks do not exist, simply that they are not formally recognized. Possibly this is because feedback is undervalued or it is assumed that informal networking is sufficient and will happen anyway without having to be planned. Similarly, the policy-making element may be visible, but may only be loosely connected to the whole structure; or it has developed a will of its own and has disappeared, or been hijacked, to fulfil some other mission. The model exists, in other words, but looks neglected, like a dismembered bicycle, still firmly locked to a community railing, but unfortunately no longer functional.

Coordinating structures in relation to 'through the net' children within schools depend much on local interpretations of education policy. In education, for example, it has been agency policy since the passing of the 1981 Education Act to encourage the inclusion in mainstream schools of children with special educational needs across a wide range of difficulties, and *intra*-agency, multidisciplinary teams have been developed in many schools and LEAs as a strategy to promote inclusion. For some young people, however, the principle of inclusion requires not only that services are effectively coordinated within agencies but also that they are linked to an equally effectively coordinated inter-agency structure. The case studies of individuals demonstrate what happens if this does not exist. Where no inter-agency team or panel exists, to whom agency practitioners can refer those at risk of falling 'through the net', responsibility remains either with a lone practitioner or with someone who has assumed this role voluntarily, or with no one. From the point of view of the young person, the risks in this situation can be, as the case studies demonstrated, to life and/or to life chances by failing 'to become integrated into a normally accepted pattern of social responsibility, particularly with regard to work and adult life' (OECD 1995: 3). The Warnock Report (1978: para. 1.4) expresses this risk in similar terms, as the failure 'to enter the world after formal education is over as an active participant in society and a responsible contributor to it, capable of achieving as much independence as possible.'

From the point of view of the agencies, failure to meet the needs of 'at risk' people is compounded by the risk that they, the agencies, are then exposed to in terms of loss of public recognition and support, professional and agency morale and self-esteem. These risks, for client, professional and agency, are not trivial. Avoiding them, however, may appear to agencies to involve them in activities which may not seem important enough to bother about (networks), or, conversely, seem too expensive and/or threatening to contemplate (inter-agency teams).

Teams and networks

Teams, whether intra- or inter-agency, are often the most visible point of contact and comparison between agencies. If we accept that teams do not stand alone, and that it is the effective functioning of the model as a whole which matters most, it is appropriate to examine, first, their function in general, and in their relationship with networks, and, second, how teams operate within agencies, of which the example chosen here is the typical secondary school special educational needs team.

In some situations, depending on the context and working methods, it may not be easy to distinguish between teams and networks, especially in a small school or service. It is an important distinction nonetheless. Although membership is unlikely to be mutually exclusive and there will many opportunities for overlap, they serve different purposes. Kanter (1984: 166) sees the team as one of a number of network-forming devices encouraging 'the immediate exchange of support and information and [creating] contact to be drawn on in the future.' According to Kanter (p.166), innovative companies:

> make the assignments with the most critical change implications to teams across areas rather than to individuals or segmented units . . . Such

formal teams, not incidentally, served as models of the method that top management endorsed for carrying out major tasks and projects.

This is not a new phenomenon, she notes, nor will *any* team help innovation. In her experience of older established industries, 'integrative team mechanisms may account for successful problem solving and innovation' (p. 167). Teams that achieved this, however, drew members from 'a diversity of sources, a variety of areas'. Innovating companies seem deliberately to create a 'market place of ideas', recognizing that a multiplicity of points of view need to be brought to bear on a problem (p. 167).

Kingdon (1992: 142), discussing teams and networks in the human services, stresses that it is 'important to distinguish between them as both are essential in providing a balanced package of care to most individuals.' In the complex multidisciplinary world developing in, for example, social work and health in the 1980s it was being recognized, however, that:

> Intensive multi-disciplinary teamwork is a way of working which needs to be used sparingly and concentrated where it can yield highest returns. For the most part we need to consider ways of achieving a fair level of effectiveness in a wide range of looser and more spasmodic interrelationships.
>
> (Webb 1982: 11)

Webb's view was that whatever these interrelationships were, they were necessary in order to 'galvanise particular sets of workers into closer interaction at points where a breakdown of communication and joint action would be disastrous' (p. 11). Muir (1984) draws attention to Hey's (1979) distinction between teams and networks. Thus a *team* is described as the 'continuing interaction between a small clearly bounded group of the same people who share a common task, similar values and who hold distinctive knowledge and skills' (Muir 1984: 170). Muir points out that 'if there are no common objectives or pooling of skills then it is unlikely that teamwork exists' (p. 168). A *network* is 'composed of a range of people with different knowledge and skills who may meet infrequently with a changing constituency, yet who work on a common task when the occasion demands' (p. 170).

Both types of collaboration characterized the ECST as it developed from 1988. Interestingly, their 'network' predated the team by some years and was regarded as good in itself, with an important role to fulfil. It had also, as was the case with Elmore III, developed, over a period of years, a climate of confidence and trust in which new initiatives could flourish. In the early 1980s, any role that it might play in an overarching inter-agency structure was not, of course apparent, since there was no team as yet to which it could relate.

From the standpoint of the agency or organization, Payne (1982: 13) comments 'that teamwork . . . is an instrument for carrying out the policy of the agency'. As such, teams are subsets of a larger organization. Therefore, he suggests, it is necessary to look at the total structure and goals of the host organization in order to understand the functioning of a team within the larger system. Payne stresses 'the importance of setting up a clear system for collaboration in a multi-disciplinary team, the clear differentiation of tasks . . . and respect for the values of other occupational groups' (p. 107). This emphasis on the relationship between team and organizational purpose foreshadows the emphasis placed ten years later, by researchers such as Huxham and Macdonald (1992), on the importance of making aims and values explicit in order to achieve the benefits of collaboration.

The management and training of teams has attracted an extensive literature, some of which is relevant to inter-agency working. Only recently, however, has this extended beyond the world of professionals. In the literature of the 1980s and early 1990s the focus was on professionals and their training for inter-professional practice, some of which might take place in inter-professional teams (Higgins and Jaques 1986; Becher 1994). Others are concerned with the training of professionals for inter-professional practice, as agency members, but not necessarily as members of inter-agency teams (Bines 1992). By contrast, teams, such as youth offending teams, that grew up during the 1990s can be described more accurately as teams of inter-*agency* practitioners. In education, for example, Thomas (1992), Lacey and Lomas (1993), Solity and Bickler (1994) and Lacey (2001) recognize the range of people from different parts of disciplinary and agency hierarchies who now make up intra- and inter-agency teams.

Owen (1996: 17), discussing the reasons for the prevalence of teams in modern organizations, claims that 'For a long time, business gurus have been saying that staid, difficult to respond hierarchies are out and fast, flexible, flatter networks in . . . Yet the move from hierarchical organisations has been slow. Many use this network description, but few have yet to make it a reality for all who work in the organisation.' The hierarchical mentality is hard to shift, in which managers see power as a limited rather than an expanding resource and therefore fear its loss through networking. For Owen, 'The clearest difference between a hierarchy and a network organisation is that a network is more flexible and can respond quicker, which is vital today' (p. 18). Although networks look different from hierarchies, 'the differences are not just structural' (p. 18). There may, for example, be gender differences in management. Owen quotes Helgesen's view that women managers tend to:

> structure organisations as a web, or network, rather than a hierarchy . . . Each of the women described her place in the organisation as being in the centre reaching out, rather than at the top reaching down. A hierarchy focuses on targeting a position, climbing the ladder and knocking out competition. A web emphasizes interrelationships, building up strength and knitting loose ends into the fabric.
>
> (p. 20)

Pondering the changes she observed as a management consultant, Owen considers 'The old ways won't work. Confrontation has been replaced by co-operation, and teams are working across these companies' (p. 17). Was it, she asks, because in industry managers had their backs to the wall and were being forced to change, or was it that 'workers are participating in the deci-sions and problems in these companies and feel part of a team?' (p. 17). Her interest in teams led her to study the Red Arrows to explore 'their *approach* to teamwork and *process*' (p. 24), and the notion that by doing one's best for the team, one is also doing the best for oneself.

Developing teams, Owen maintains, means developing organizations, since teams are not isolated and have to interact with others in the organization: 'leadership and teams need to be established throughout the organisation, not just at one or two levels' (p. 35). Leadership and management style emphas-izes listening, empowerment and praise. What matters more than specific skills is how managers lead and how they behave, since this affects the amount and quality of feedback they receive. Owen notes that the success of the Red Arrows lay in their ability to agree objectives and goals. They achieved this in three ways. First, they agreed objectives together, rather than assum-ing either agreement and commitment, or that goals were preordained and did not need discussion. In work with people 'at risk' this is important, since, as the case studies of young people show, agency commitment cannot be assumed.

Second, the Red Arrows set performance targets and objectives based on what they intended to achieve, rather than simply on what things they would do (p. 124). They used 'the results of monitoring by feedback to tell people what they have achieved and set new goals, or assess why goals were not achieved', and then took action to ensure further success (p. 86). In the context of children and young people, the emphasis on achievable goals, monitoring and evaluation before the setting of fresh targets is an essential part of effective case management. Asking participants to focus on what they can expect to achieve rather than on what they undertake to do has consid-erable implications for the running of case and team meetings.

Third, the Red Arrows were careful to elicit individual goals from team members and to incorporate (or discover) these in the team goals. In this way team synergy was multiplied and commitment and high performance from all its members were guaranteed. In the case of the Red Arrows, this was important because the enterprise is inherently risky, requiring daring and consummate skill. Again, the comparison with working with 'at risk' people makes Owen's analysis particularly apt.

In contrast to teams, networks have, until relatively recently, received little attention from researchers. According to McCabe *et al.* (1997: 1), 'Partner-ships and networks have become a prominent feature of the way in which voluntary, community and public organisations operate.' They define part-nerships as 'formal relationships between agencies, for example a board or company. They have fixed memberships and clear boundaries' (p. 1). They define networks as operating 'through relationships between individuals with shared interests, values or goals. They tend to have indistinct boundaries and fluid memberships' (p. 1). In relation to power, McCabe *et al.* consider that while networks are frequently described as 'flat' relationships between indi-viduals and/or organizations, partnerships are associated with hierarchical structures which are less inclined to share power.

By comparison with the accounts, in Elmore I and II, of networking associated with 'difficult to place' adults and 'through the net' young people, McCabe *et al.* (1997) are less interested in the potential of networking as a generator of feedback, as a venue for senior managers to meet practitioners, or for provider to meet purchaser. Nor, in their study, is the network's power to influence fully acknowledged, nor the skills required of the network broker. In relation to 'difficult to place' adults, these skills proved to be core inter-agency skills. They were just as useful when transferred for the benefit of those working with 'through the net' young people in Elmore II and III. In this study networks are seen as an integral, if neglected, part of organizational structures, providing the feedback to inform and evaluate inter-agency meta-strategy, as well as the agency strategy.

The role of the coordinator in the management of change

Writers on the subject of teams devote considerable attention to team leadership. Lacey and Lomas (1993: 144) consider that the team leader gives 'direction and moulds the individual parts into a whole'. It can also be their job to make final decisions. In an inter-professional team, Higgins and Jaques (1986: 8) raise the issue of who, in a team stressing equality and collegiality, should lead. In consequence, 'some regard the question of "leadership" as outmoded.' These issues are all affected by the culture of change, which, as in the business world, is required in the provision of human services. To be an individual 'at risk' is to be exceptionally vulnerable to negative change and exceptionally in need of positive change. Kanter (1984: 289) identifies five key 'building blocks of change'. These are:

- departures from tradition;
- crisis or galvanizing effect;
- strategic decisions;
- individual 'prime movers';
- action 'vehicles'.

The first two, according to Kanter, will not of themselves guarantee change. Leadership is required to make strategic decisions in favour of change and create 'an orderly plan' (p. 294). These plans then need prime movers and mechanisms with structures and procedures which will enable the innovation to work in practice.

The case studies considered in Chapter 7 suggest that to work with people who are 'at risk' requires a departure from tradition. Unlike a business, agency enterprise in this context does not necessarily fail if clients are lost. The galvanizing effect of a crisis is then less marked. In this situation, the attitudes, beliefs and priorities of leaders and prime movers become relatively more important. For Kanter, coordination and the role of the coordinator have, as the result of changed attitudes and assumptions about how organizations change and grow, become more, rather than less, significant. The assumption used to be, according to Kanter, that organizations consisted of specialisms, coordination was itself a specialism and coordinators made sure, as managers, that the parts fitted together. In the new approach, coordination is more complex. Even if efforts are made to reduce specialization, organizations:

> have responsibilities for the consequences of their actions beyond their own borders. They need to learn about and stay informed about what is happening elsewhere, and they need to honor their social responsibilities to act for the larger good. These tasks call for managers with general perspectives and with experience of more than one function.
>
> (Kanter 1984: 61)

Handy (1985: 210) considers that 'the greater the differentiation the greater the potential for conflict' and cites coordination and the role of coordinator as one of a range of integrating devices to overcome these difficulties. He considers that 'the greater the degree of differentiation between the cultures the more devices the organisation should use' (p. 210). He acknowledges that the role is a difficult one and suggests devices, of which coordinators need some or all to fulfil the role. These are:

1 Position power and the appropriate status.
2 Expert power, and being perceived to have it by all the groups or individuals whom he or she is coordinating. Experience both sides of the fence.
3 Interpersonal skills necessary to resolve conflict situations between individuals in a problem-solving mode.

Team synergy thus seems to rest in the coordinating skills of the team leader, who in turn depends on guidance from senior managers in the organization, who must then, in Kanter's (1984: 61) phrase, 'honor their social responsibilities to act for the larger good' by ensuring that the work of the teams for which they are responsible does not undermine, or conflict with, the work of similar teams in other agencies.

Special educational needs teams in mainstream schools

Teams of interest to this study are those specifically designed to:

- Help agencies to support individuals at risk of falling 'through the net' to remain within agency support networks.
- Help to change those elements in the environment which create difficulties for individuals.

There are many examples within agencies serving young people: health service paediatric assessment teams; GP practices; social services adolescent services teams; LEA special educational needs support services (SENSS); education social work teams. In most cases referral to these teams requires only intra-agency intervention, even though the initial referral may have been prompted by another agency. For example, referral to a GP might be suggested by a school as a way of accessing adolescent mental health services, or a referral to social services might come via an educational social worker. The majority of referrals to primary care services are straightforward and require only minimal inter-agency cooperation. However, crisis may be only one step away, and a successful outcome may depend on the existence of effective coordination within agencies, as well as between them and the development of the roles outlined in Chapter 7.

School models of cooperation

Schools can be regarded, for the present purpose, as microcosms of society with their own collection of 'agencies', in the form of faculty and year teams, their own networking possibilities and a senior management policy-making group. Prominent in the model (and variously labelled) are special needs, learning, curriculum or pupil support teams playing the role, in this analogy, of the 'inter-agency' team. In schools committed to inclusion, these teams perform in much the same manner as an inter-agency team working between actual agencies. They may have set up centres which act as a 'holding bay' between the classroom and home or street, and take referrals from colleagues in any part of the school system needing support. Young people at risk of falling 'through the net', or those returning to school from a period of exclusion or illness, can receive immediate support from skilled staff with time to listen. Team members, as network brokers, coordinate existing school resources and mobilize additional resources from other agencies or the local community, provide key workers and undertake independent assessment. The team itself will be supported by senior management within the school, and there may well be a formal network, such as a school liaison group. There may be links with a partnership of schools or with a community network. As with the examples of inter-agency projects described above, special needs teams operating within schools in this manner share many of the characteristics of good practice noted in inter-agency teams. There is the same emphasis on, for example, commitment and support from senior management, networking and regular inter-agency meetings to discuss ethical issues, changes in legislation and practice, gaps in provision and information sharing, common work practices, agreed definitions and joint training. There is, too, the same tension between upstream and downstream work expressed in the well-known dilemma of the SENCO, caught among the piles of paperwork, meetings and telephone calls accumulating around case work and the need for change in the school environment. It is interesting that the need for a balance between upstream and downstream work was implied in the five key functions of the *Role of the Remedial Teacher* soon after the publication of the Warnock Report (NARE 1979) and that this feature of the role lives on in similar functions set out in the revised Code of Practice (DfES 2001c). SENCOs and their teams therefore understand as much as anyone the importance of coordinating structures and of maintaining systems to promote the circulation of feedback. None the less, the tension between the need for whole school change and the demands of case management is reflected in what continues to be a strong tendency within school to focus on the needs of specific individuals or groups rather than on whole-school development. There is also the same reluctance, noted above, to redistribute resources once allocated.

However, where a balance can be held, the school model shares the advantages of the inter-agency model in its effective combination of strategy group, team and network. This enables the team to be more effective as a resource than it would have been on its own without the support of the other two elements. The team promotes effective liaison and collaboration with faculty and year teams, encouraging them to support students more fully themselves. The staff thus feel more, rather than less, skilled as a result of the team's intervention. The team can move flexibly between the other school teams to fill gaps in provision as they arise. Through its investigative and research interests the team works with others to find additional resources; for example, to negotiate funding and staff for new projects to meet unexpected needs and needs previously unidentified. The team is also able to advise on long-term strategic planning. Finally, the team coordinator is able to arrange regular network meetings to promote further collaborative work, to maintain an overview of the provision available and as a vehicle for feedback.

For individual young people, the model provides support enabling them to remain in school if attendance is at risk, or return to school if they have been away. Continuity of support is also guaranteed. Where a wider, inter-agency network in the community exists (as it did in Elmore III), the team can, by tapping into that network, plan, together with other agencies, more effective packages of support than they would otherwise have been able to do. There are particular strengths, especially for small secondary and primary schools, if existing partnerships of schools (Lunt *et al.* 1994) can be further developed in the manner of Elmore III. As a strategy this helps, for example, SENCOs in primary schools, who may be fulfilling the role for no more than an hour a week, to recognize that they too are part of a local 'team', involving members of the LEA SENSS and support staff, and have access to a 'network' which might include parents, governors and local community leaders. Both team and network, however tenuous, once recognized, can be cultivated.

Refocusing energy and redistributing resources to support joined up action

One response to the problem of agency failure to support those with needs requiring the services of more than one agency has been, as we have seen, to set up an independent inter-agency team or panel to undertake case management and network-broking. These projects have typically depended on the vision and commitment of an influential individual, charity or research body. The result, in some instances, has been that at the end of the pilot period, agency funding has replaced the original grant and the work becomes absorbed into agency practice. The ECST, MARS and Surrey Youth Link were early examples of projects which were able to convince policy-makers, through practice, in a way rhetoric could not have done. The result could then be described as a refocusing of agency energy and redistribution of resources to the least advantaged.

The study of young people 'through the net' is more than usually instructive for SENCOs, since these young people do not fit typical descriptors of educational need any more than they fit the descriptors for other agencies. Young people 'through' the education 'net' also move from category to category and cannot be compartmentalized. In the container metaphor they are butterflies or very slippery fish, rarely staying still long enough to be examined. Those who work with them have to be prepared to enter the rough ground between agency playing fields in order to observe, meet and talk with them. This is especially true of teenagers, who pass rapidly out of the knowledge of the one agency, education, that would see them daily. In interview, however, individuals 'through the net' can, by expressing their needs and feelings, reveal what provision is needed for everyone more accurately than anyone else. To ignore them as 'exceptions that prove the rule', or as 'too difficult to be worth helping', is to ignore an opportunity to learn how to adapt the environment in ways which, by definition, will benefit everyone, and to raise expectations of what is possible and how success can be achieved. An example of the way in which coordinating models enable agencies to build on such insights and refocus and redistribute resources is given by current approaches to funding special educational needs in school.

A number of studies over the past ten years have discussed and/or have proposed funding mechanisms to ensure that mainstream schools identify children's special educational needs and arrange provision for them in accordance with the principles and practice of inclusion (Audit Commission 1992a, 1998; Coopers and Lybrand 1996; Meijer 1999; Evans et al. 2001). Evidence from some LEAs suggests that how funding is used, how support is organized and the way in which an LEA's concept of special educational needs is interpreted can be more important than how much funding there is overall and how equitably it is distributed (Gray and Dessent 1993). Greater correspondence between needs and funding is desirable but 100 per cent accuracy is not realistic and, if pursued too far as a goal, distracts from the primary purpose, which is to ensure that existing resources are used efficiently for the children and young people who need them most.

An NFER study (1997) points out that local management of schools (LMS) and the 1994 Code of Practice emphasize identification and assessment of the individual child's learning difficulties rather than consideration of wider issues, such as school effectiveness and teacher effectiveness. Thus headteachers tend to request equity, efficiency and transparency based on the idea that x needs should equal y funds. This has turned out to be an oversimplistic and flawed relationship. It is essential, therefore, that funding follows existing good practice and attempts to improve practice, rather than simple identification of need. Schools tend to want, and think they need, a change of funding, when, in fact, what they need, but do not necessarily want, is a change in organization and practice.

Effective SEN funding mechanisms are still at an early stage of development and there is, as yet, little agreement or consistency among LEAs as to best practice. Although research evidence to support particular approaches is, likewise, still developing, some LEAs have been successful in combining low levels of 'statementing' with maximum financial delegation (Gray and Dessent 1993; Beek 2002; Gray 2001). The common factors in these LEAs are:

• Special attention is given to the role, coordination and delegation of LEA SENSS (Gray 2001).
• Communication between individuals (e.g. school SENCO and LEA officer) and 'paper' meetings are replaced by round table conferences attended by representatives of all the relevant services. This promotes transparency by allowing issues to be discussed openly and good practice shared (Kahn 2002).
• A balance is held at all levels between issues-led 'upstream' research and development, and needs-led 'downstream' decision-making.
• Schools are reminded of their responsibilities towards their pupils with SEN. This is achieved through their regular meetings with SENSS where they are also offered practical support and guidance.

It is particularly important, therefore, as the strategy element in the structure, that LEAs:

• Clarify their concept of inclusive education.
• Clarify the role and organization of SENSS and its relationship to the schools and to LEA officers and advisers.
• Use existing intra-agency structures to best effect; for example, school partnerships (Cade and Caffyn 1994; Lunt et al. 1994)
• Adapt their LMS scheme so that it integrates upstream and downstream work.

Effective models can be illustrated diagrammatically (Figure 8.1) and reveal the elements of policy-making group, team and network similar to those found in the inter-agency model devised from Elmore and discussed in Chapter 6.

In these models good practice is identified and assessed, rather than individuals, and interest focuses on the most complex because of what can be learnt there about how to improve practice for everyone. Almost invariably, as many practitioners will attest (Nind and Hewitt 1994; Hart 1996), to accept the challenge of individuals whose needs are complex is to be rewarded with a dynamic catalyst for change. By working together, members of a school consultation group can exert more influence to support schools in refocusing policy and purpose to include the 'difficult to include' than any individual member of it could on their own. Where the traditional power and authority of the institution is obstructing the move towards more inclusive practice this may be the best way forward. In some LEAs, for example, some funding for SEN is distributed on the basis of an annual audit of individual pupils' needs. Annual meetings in which the SENCOs, perhaps in

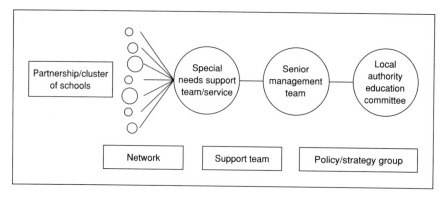

Figure 8.1   Integration of upstream and downstream processes: LEA special needs support service

a school partnership, meet with members of SENSS to moderate their assessment of their school's student needs have proved their worth in terms of staff development, identification of good practice, early intervention strategies, training needs and gaps in provision. In this respect the participants experience some of the benefits of a formal network and this mitigates the disadvantages of the more bureaucratic aspects of pupil audit as a means of distributing scarce resources. In these meetings, too, the group facilitators function (and have similar duties) in ways reminiscent of network minders, as the following comments indicate (Roaf 1999a). The role of facilitator, in this example, had been 'important in preventing decisions from being made on the previous experience of teachers and SENCOs rather than on objective information.' Facilitators reported that:

SENCOs/headteachers enjoyed the chance to look at other schools' practice. They began to appreciate how difficult it can be for outside professionals to work out the problem if the evidence is poor.

The process [moderation] was viewed very positively as an effective learning experience as well as a fair process.

A number of SENCOs said they will change the way they do things as a result of moderation . . . It will be valuable to go through the process annually, involving all schools. This would lead to faster professional development as schools worked together and looked critically at each other's practice. The process was seen as valuable in itself, quite apart from helping to ensure fairer deployment of resources.

For the SENCOs, moderation provided: 'a good INSET opportunity . . . don't feel you are working in isolation' . . . 'Plenty of focused discussion. An afternoon a year like this one would be good – just to keep everyone reassured that they're doing it right.'

In some LEAs, such as Northamptonshire and Nottinghamshire, SENNS and schools have been working together for years, while others have adopted the approach more recently. Kahn (2002) records high levels of satisfaction in her account of Norfolk's collaborative monitoring process for SEN. These experiences suggest that the inter-personal and inter-professional skills required for inter-agency network broking and network minding can be fostered and learnt in the more familiar, less challenging world within agencies.

Conclusion

Coordinating structures within agencies are required:

- to clarify and assert agency policy;
- to use knowledge about the needs of the most complex to identify good practice and suggest improvements to meet community needs as well as individual needs;
- to reprioritize energy and resources;
- to combine skills and resources effectively;
- to encourage feedback;
- to identify areas for research and development;
- to monitor and evaluate progress.

Looking for points of comparison between a mainstream school's special needs team and similar teams in other services highlights some other points of contrast between client group, agency priorities and definitions of people regarded as 'at risk'. Where inter-agency and intra-agency teams exist for people 'at risk', they are an indication that a coordinating structure also exists, even if only in a shadowy form. There may well be a network but the likelihood is that it will be informal and that precious feedback will be draining out of the system rather than bringing new life into it. Examples from inter-agency practice support the view developed in this study that intra-agency teams supporting people 'at risk' need to be connected to:

1 *Intra*-agency structures in which policy and networking groups are formally identified and supported.
2 *Inter*-agency teams and networks functioning within an inter-agency coordinating structure designed to support children and young people at risk of falling 'through the net'.

The challenge now is to consider how recent government-supported inter-agency agencies are to be linked with existing intra-agency structures and their as yet informal networks. Letting a thousand 'inter-agency agency' flowers bloom as a strategy to prevent children and young people falling 'through the net' will only be effective within a fully coordinated structure allowing feedback to flow freely through the system.

CHAPTER NINE

Coordinating services to promote inclusion

Over the period covered in this book, a cyclical pattern emerges. The post-Second World War welfare model of universal provision persisted into the 1960s. In this climate, if needs existed, it was assumed that they should be met and that post-war growth and prosperity would eventually achieve this. In the face of deepening recession, universal provision as an ideal became more difficult to sustain and led to calls for greater accountability. 'Accountability' in this context leads inexorably to identification and assessment of individual need at the expense of universal provision. Hence priorities are set so that agencies focus on ever reducing numbers of individuals in more extreme need. Ironically, the equal opportunities debate may have contributed indirectly to these developments during the 1970s and 1980s. A social justice model based on positive action alone is an approach to the problem of inequality based on rights rather than needs: the ideal of universal provision is easily neglected, and downstream prevails over upstream. What is required is a strategy in which upstream/downstream and needs/rights are held in equilibrium. In the absence of such a strategy, practitioners lurch from one mode to the other with no means of creating a balance between them.

Over the same period, inter-agency work itself, and the study of it, is revealed as having a longer history than is sometimes supposed. Practitioners frequently had personal experience of inter-agency cooperation at earlier stages of their working lives. Thus social workers, youth workers, probation officers or teachers, even when dominated in the 1990s by downstream work, often mentioned in discussion their previous involvement with upstream initiatives such as intermediate treatment. They used this experience as a point of reference when considering the benefits of inter-agency work, but had not considered how the organizational and coordinating structures familiar to them within agencies might be translated into structures which would function between them.

The dilemma practitioners faced in relation to upstream–downstream options was revealed in Elmore II, for example, in the significance of the relationship between individuals in need, and the strength of feeling these needs aroused in individual practitioners. This relationship could be most sharply observed when practitioners were faced with individuals for whom they required the help of one or more other agencies but had no means of securing this. The practitioner could then, according to their personality and/or professional circumstances, give up, ignore this situation or persist in the attempt to find some means of crossing agency boundaries. Generally they stayed in downstream mode and looked for a short-term solution, perhaps seeking the help of someone known personally to them in another agency.

The Elmore model attempts to help agencies and practitioners to resolve this dilemma by developing a structure allowing them to move into long-term upstream mode through, rather than as an alternative to, the support of downstream work. Evidence from other sources in the business world and systemic work with organizations suggested that coordinating structures were required principally to ensure that 'the life blood' of feedback flowed freely through the system, within and between all levels in agency hierarchies. Although the word 'hierarchy' is used, this did not imply a hierarchical mode of operation. Instead it reflected the qualitative differences between thought, action and communication. Everyone coordinates these activities naturally, but coordination for the organizational body as a whole has to be achieved artificially; hence the need for a structure. Maintaining a structure to allow the free flow of feedback required new roles and responsibilities and the reinterpretation of long familiar roles. None the less, the structure itself appeared to be successful because it was simple, enabling even the smallest action carried out by para-professionals working far from an agency base to connect with managers and policy-makers in its effects. Matters of judgement, decision-making and responsibility – the ability to 'do the right thing, at the right time, for the right reason' – assumed a new significance for everyone involved.

Factors contributing to successful inter-agency work

The historical overview and the case studies of projects and individuals suggested that the factors contributing to successful inter-agency work covered four main areas: legislation, organization, professional practice and resources. Some conclusions relating to these factors are summarized here.

Legislators have it in their power to set up inter-departmental coordinating structures and joint funding mechanisms. They also have it in their power to ensure that strategies to meet children's needs address them as a group with collective needs as citizens, as well as with individual needs arising from particular circumstances. This is not to say that legislation is not also needed to cover specific groups of children in, for example, hospital, residential care or custody, or those who are homeless, but legislation should also devise effective government structures which do not compartmentalize children and ensure that preventative and proactive work is fully integrated.

In terms of *structures and organization*, when things went wrong in the life of a young person, as a consequence of the failure of agencies to cooperate, incidents in the 'chain of causation' could be plotted on a grid and this helped to reveal where the difficulties lay. Detailed analysis could then be used to point to improvements that would have to be made to prevent a similar occurrence. In demanding cases, the grid could also be used as a preventative strategy to highlight areas of risk from factors already known. When practitioners had been successful in retaining young people within agency support networks this analysis was also helpful. Models 'fit for the purpose' seemed to be those in which system and process were closely linked.

Structures within and between agencies can, in principle, be set up without legislation, but this has been rare. Where they exist between agencies, it is as a result of legislation; for example, the Scottish Children's Hearing, multiprofessional assessment, joint consultative committees and area child protection committees. How effective they are, and how ready to adapt to changing ideas and circumstances, depends, however, on improved coordination elsewhere in the system. The development of initiatives such as Sure Start and Connexions, as responses to calls for joined up thinking, likewise depends on effective coordination and network-broking elsewhere in the system, particularly within agencies. Without that safeguard, large-scale inter-agency agencies run the risk of funnelling young people out of primary care agencies rather than helping these agencies to become more inclusive. Similarly, if inter-agency agencies are not connected to an inter-agency network, the lifeblood of feedback is lost to the system. In general, on the evidence presented here, policy-makers and managers suffer from lack of feedback, yet such a loss puts progress as a flexible 'learning organization' (Senge 1999) in jeopardy.

The evidence presented in this study suggests that without the practitioner network, the element which most powerfully generates feedback, agencies cannot 'learn'. This makes it difficult for them to achieve their objectives, among which is the intention to maintain children and young people within agency support networks. Thus although frameworks for effective models of cooperation exist, especially within agencies, they tend to lie unnoticed, with key components, most commonly the network, neglected and undeveloped. In the school model, it is proposed here that SEN teams consider the role of 'tight' steering, or review, groups as well as 'loose' networks to help them to sustain the balance between upstream and downstream work. In the overall structure a small steering group, with membership representative of the relevant agencies, functioned as the 'brain' of the system (Glenny 2000). Within schools, for example, such a group can support SENCOs in keeping a balance between preventative work and case work when they might be under pressure to do otherwise. Typically, debate will be about how and when it is appropriate to focus on the margins, or to shed work which can be safely left in the hands of mainstream colleagues.

In relation to *professional practice,* inter-personal skills emerged as the most important of the core skills required by those engaging in inter-agency work, coupled with what Handy (1985) refers to as 'position power' (status) and 'expert power': a working knowledge of the range of working practice, legislation and culture of the agencies and professionals involved with the client group. Inter-agency work now emerges (and with much less suspicion than formerly), as a new area of professionalism and specialist expertise. The roles required to maintain an effective structure, within which joined up action can take place, involve the ability to act as key workers, independent assessors and network minders and brokers. Those fulfilling these roles must also be able to identify gaps in provision, to frame research proposals and to facilitate research. Members of inter-agency teams also have a key role in designing and leading inter- and intra-agency staff development and training to address issues arising from the network. As any school SENCO or learning support assistant will confirm, the idea that inter-agency activity might blur boundaries or detract from specialist expertise is potentially threatening to professionals. Highly specialized professionals are valued for their specialist skill, not necessarily for their ability to cooperate. Networkers and coordinators are required to harness this expertise, secure access for those who need it and mediate professional expertise for their clients. Increasingly, however, professionals in all agencies now work alongside para-professionals as fellow team members. This has increased the responsibilities of intra-agency team leaders, now more involved with personnel issues, training, staff development and research than formerly. Similarly, in inter-agency work, inter- and intra-agency para-professionals are beginning to appear in, for example, schools or children's homes, sharing many skills in common the closer they are to agency boundaries.

Finally, in this discussion of key factors contributing to successful inter-agency work it is suggested that one of the most significant measures of success is the extent to which experience of inter-agency work persuades agencies to refocus agency purpose and redistribute agency *resources* towards inclusion. Putting resources into focused joined up action, of the kind promoted by Elmore-type models, allows agencies to evaluate current agency practice and provision as a joint exercise. It does not necessarily remove the resource from 'mainstream' resources; instead it refocuses that universal resource in a manner more likely to promote inclusion as a principle. In this way, as Owen (1996) established in relation to individual members of teams, the goals of the school's SEN team can be realized in the school's goals for inclusion. Inter-agency panels or support teams taking referrals from agencies of individuals at points of crisis or change are thus, in effect, acting as peer moderators and evaluators of agency practice. Developing approaches to the methods by which resources for special educational needs are distributed in mainstream schools illustrate the point being made here (Beek 2002; Kahn 2002). Scrutiny of the individuals referred shifts the container metaphor implied in the phrase 'through the net', so that practitioners become enquirers and investigators rather than hunters and trappers, more interested in releasing their clients into a friendly environment than protecting them from a hostile one. It then becomes clear that it is practitioners who are trapped by the failure of agencies to cooperate rather than their clients, and that it is problems, notably the 'wicked issues' referred to above, not people, that fall 'through the net'.

The way ahead

In the field of joined up action there is no shortage of ideas for further debate and research and some are suggested here.

The inter-agency coordinating model presented here as an evaluation and training tool now needs to be tested more widely and used:

- with other constellations of agencies and different client groups;
- within agencies.

If, as is suggested here, the structure is successful in redistributing resources towards the most vulnerable, it would be useful to compare this model of cooperation with those used by non-government organizations such as Oxfam or WaterAid. Amnesty International is an obvious example, with its network of letter writers and its ability to transform the effort of many powerless individuals into an organization with a powerful influence.

The problem of how to organize services for children is likely to be a matter for continued debate, and will especially focus on the relationship between primary care agencies and the many small- and large-scale private and public sector initiatives for children and young people coexisting with them. Hertfordshire's merger between education and social services is at a very early stage, and developments there will be of great interest to researchers. It remains a matter for debate as to whether it is either feasible or desirable to plan for services entirely without boundaries in the increasingly specialized and predominantly urban environment of modern times. Even if primary care services for children do become more fully integrated, there is still the potential difficulty of crossing the boundary between child and adult and of what is offered to children independently of their families. Underlying these concerns is the fact that no local or national government department is exempt from a responsibility for the welfare of children (Payne 2002). The evidence from the projects outlined here, and past history, suggests that boundaries continue to be, for all practical purposes, a given. The majority are not adversely affected by the existence of boundaries provided that the services closest to them in their communities work together effectively.

This study has therefore focused on how agencies as a whole ensure the provision of coordinated services to local communities, however remote or deprived those communities are. This line of argument sets up slightly different questions. Do, for example, inter-agency workers build bridges or demolish barriers? The meta-narrative in this study has been about the design and maintenance of sustainable local and national inter-agency structures and practice which will ensure safe boundary crossings. Does a barrier matter if it can be crossed safely? Western minds rooted in Aristotelian thought tend to think in bipolar terms of A and not-A, this or that, where Eastern thought rooted in Buddhism might be more at home with merged services and more communitarian approaches (Kosko 1993).

These ideas merit more detailed comparative study internationally. The reality for the individual 'through the net' people who feature in this study is that we are usually thinking in terms of barriers rather than bridges. As the mother said of agency behaviour over the referral of her 14-year-old son, 'we were like tennis balls' – lobbed out of the relative safety of agency playing fields into the rough ground beyond. With this image in mind, my own opinion, influenced by researchers such as Hodgkin and Newell (1996), Moss and Petrie (1997) and Newell (2000), is that if highly skilled practitioners, working within an inter-agency framework, are the best hope of retrieving children from that rough ground, then this is a task for which a Children's Unit at Cabinet Office level with an independent Children's Rights Commissioner could provide the necessary leadership, vision and authority. Consideration of the needs and rights of children impacts on so many government departments that it is difficult to see how a single Ministry of Children could achieve as much as a small 'inter-agency' group at that level, fulfilling the roles identified above on the ground, but this time fulfilling them in relation to the impact of government policy.

Primary care agencies may be unwieldy and 'slow learning' but they have the advantage of a wealth of professional expertise. An advantage of firm boundaries is that equally firm bridges can be built joining them. The argument here has been for some clarity about what those bridges look like and what traffic is to cross them. In the 1980s some commentators (Payne 1982; Webb 1982; Muir 1984) seemed to suggest that inter-agency work should be used sparingly and in carefully focused projects. The Elmore model appears to support this view. This approach uses small inter-agency teams able, in effect, to explore unknown territory between agency boundaries and bring back information from which mainstream agencies can 'learn' new ways. This still seems to be a worthy ambition, more likely to promote inclusive communities than the creation of large inter-agency agencies which run the risk of appearing to dismiss primary care agencies as incapable of learning. Even in the case of the most likely candidates for amalgamation, between education and social services, as in Hertfordshire's recent example, the question of the relationship with other agencies remains.

A major problem, mentioned in this study but unresolved, is to understand 'how agencies can be encouraged to co-operate effectively when their fundamental tenets are in opposition' (Roaf 2001: 181). Of the three primary care agencies, social services and health present as protectors of life and life chances. Education does not.

Education's objectives, intensified in school, have traditionally been based on concepts of excellence and norms which depend on abstractions, ideas of what can be achieved by some, and of what behaviours are to count as normal and manageable. Until relatively recently, the school system as a whole was designed to select out those who do not conform and whose life chances were then, by definitioin, most at risk.

(p. 181)

This still applies: for some, life chances continue to be exposed, metaphorically speaking, to the elements.

Nor are the distinctions and links between upstream and downstream work clearly articulated. Local inter-agency coordinating groups such as those described in Elmore III, in which young people also play their part, have an important role in helping all services to support each other in becoming more inclusive. Unless they become so, practitioners close to those whose promise is most at risk will continue to feel that they too have been exposed to the elements.

A feature of joined up action concerns the natural tendency to focus on downstream work at the expense of upstream work. This appears to be deeply ingrained, and for good reason where there is an individual in crisis. Possibly, downstream work presents as more likely to be short term and manageable, within the capacity of individuals working on their own, whereas upstream work suggests a prolonged and difficult campaign. Attempts to address the tension between upstream and downstream, and what makes an individual or group choose one course of action over another, are particularly testing and not obviously solvable. The Elmore model was designed to introduce a mechanism allowing practitioners to get on with case management, confident that their experience would contribute to improvements for everyone.

Current thinking about children and their rights as citizens suggests that collectively, at least as much as individually, they do indeed need sustained campaigns in terms of improved quality of life: everything from amenities, such as local swimming pools, cinemas and safe cycle tracks to school, to macro issues concerning the environment, health, education and child care. On the strength of evidence presented here, inter-agency networks rooted in local communities may be the most effective bases for such campaigns, provided they seek the participation of children, young people and their families. Children and young people think more readily in terms of 'upstream' solutions than practitioners, whose tendency (and that of their jobs) is to focus on 'problems'. Current work on inclusive school design (DfES, 2001b, 2002), 'The School I'd Like' competition, which attracted 15,000 responses from young people (Birkett 2001) and moves to create a humane environment in school, in which student opinion is actively sought (Thomas and Loxley 2001), are indications of promising work in progress.

The three-tier coordinating structure in which strategy groups, teams and networks coordinate thinking, doing and communication is proposed here as a means of overcoming the worst effects of upstream/downstream, process/structure tensions. In the search for an image to portray the way in which this pattern repeats within and between agencies and in the minds of individuals, a rich source of imagery is provided by the patterns of fractal geometry, 'exhibiting structures self similar in scale' (Gleik 1988: 308), and chaos theory, in which 'Tiny differences in input could quickly become overwhelming differences in output' (p. 8). Chaos theory is uncomfortably apt in relation to DTP/TTN people at risk. The 'critical points' which make up the 'chain of causation' leading to tragedy may each in themselves be relatively insignificant, but they can have disproportionately catastrophic effects. The parallels for inter-agency work, described throughout the literature and by practitioners as 'difficult', may lie in the experience of being constantly faced with cruel dilemmas and choices over action (or more frequently, failures to act) which may have serious consequences. 'This [chaos theory] underlines even more the importance of quick learning and adjustments and of personal responsibility and opportunity. In conditions of faster change and increasing unpredictability, prompt learning and rapid adaptive responses matter even more because of the bigger later effects they can have' (Chambers 1997: 194).

Structures in which thinking, acting and communication are coordinated in a recognizable pattern repeated between and within agencies and within the practice of individuals may offer the nearest we can get to solving problems not necessarily capable of solution. On a more optimistic note, it has also been clear from this and other studies that very small positive steps, recorded by many front-line workers – perhaps taken by an 'unusual' key worker with a young person 'through the net' – can also have disproportionately positive effects.

In the introduction 'wicked issues' were discussed briefly, as complex problems all having an adverse effect on children in particular and the progress of inclusion more generally. It was suggested that addressing them required harmony between government, agency and professional purpose, since solutions involved more than one government department. It therefore seemed reasonable to suggest that a better understanding of the problems of inter-agency cooperation and coordination would contribute to the process and progress of inclusion. On the evidence presented here, this claim, I believe, is made out.

First, whether or not a boundary exists is much less important than whether it can be safely negotiated. Some boundaries become almost unnoticeable by well worn crossings, while others will always need careful negotiation through well built and maintained structures. Boundaries between agencies are not so different. This book has been an attempt to find out what such structures might look like and what roles and skills are needed to maintain them. The ten-year transition period covered in this study, from small- to large-scale inter-agency initiatives, coincides with increasing globalization and concern about the significance and interconnectednes of 'wicked issues'. It is now in everyone's interest to address these. It is not surprising, therefore, that interest in inter-agency work has grown so rapidly in recent years, now assuming status as an area of specialist expertise in its own right. 'Through the net' children and young people, because of the complexity of their needs, focus attention on the margins between agencies as no other group can. If inter-agency structures and inter-agency skills are worth having then it is with these young people that they must succeed. One of the subthemes in this study has been to sketch out what some of these structures and expertise consist of. There will almost certainly be a concern with the ability of inter-agency network brokers and 'minders' to encourage primary care agencies and their practitioners to extend their concept of inclusion and what they have it in their power to achieve with, if necessary, some additional support. There is likely to be a fundamental interest in the study of systems and process: the development of 'learning organizations' and the structuring of communication systems to promote the free flow of feedback. Inter-agency professionals will also, in their focus on marginalized communities and individuals, become knowledgeable about how the factors noted in this study concerning legislation, organizational structures, professional practice and the distribution of resources interact to inhibit or promote inclusion and equity.

Second, the closer practitioners are to the communities they serve, the greater the opportunity to cross boundaries safely. The physical building of local 'one stop shops', and of schools such as the new Millennium Primary School in Greenwich (Bishop 2001), in which the school is also the site for a number of other services for children and families are enabling in this respect. This is also how facilities for street children round the world are designed (Brink 1997). Para-professionals such as the family–school–community links worker in Elmore III illustrate the ability of such workers to pass freely between agencies and across local government boundaries. However, as the work of regional coordination partnerships for special educational needs suggests, more formal inter-agency structures are required to ensure access to specialist services for 'low incidence' needs (DfEE 1998). In these endeavours, as Elmore III demonstrated, formal local networks have the potential, as yet largely untapped, to bring local services together to identify local strengths and difficulties and suggest creative ways forward. Children and young people, however complex, international and fragmented the notion of 'community' becomes, absolutely require strong, safe, inclusive communities wherever they live. Putting their needs first would go a long way to solving 'wicked issues' for everyone. 'Through the netness' focuses attention on the role of inter-agency work to support community development and strengthens the case for the development of schools as strong integrating factors in their local communities. Some local authorities have introduced area committees as a response to recent changes in local government organization. These would appear to function as the networking element identified as the missing element in inter-agency structures and are much to be welcomed, therefore.

Finally, this study has located the difficulties agencies experience in coordinating their services effectively, in the tension between upstream and downstream work and between structure and process. The study proposes the organizational equivalent of a hub and chain on a bicycle to ensure these 'wheels' move forward in the same direction. It is suggested here that small, inter-agency initiatives operating at policy-making, implementation and networking levels within and between agencies can be that mechanism to help government, agencies and professionals to maintain their focus and coordinate their activities towards inclusion.

References

Adler, L. (1994) Introduction and overview, in *The Politics of Linking Schools and Social Services: The 1993 Yearbook of the Politics of Education Association*. London: Falmer.

Armstrong, F. and Moon, B. (1993) *Rowntree Project. Young People in Difficulties: First Year Evaluation Report*. Milton Keynes: The Open University.

Arnold, P., Bochel, H., Brodhurst, S. and Page, D. (1993) *Community Care: The Housing Dimension*. York: Joseph Rowntree Foundation.

Atkinson, M.,Wilkin, A., Stott, A. and Kinder, K. (2001) *Multi-agency Working: An Audit of Activity*. Local Government Association Research Report 17. Slough: NFER.

Audit Commission (1992a) *Getting in on the Act. Provision for Pupils with Special Needs: The National Picture*. London: HMSO.

Audit Commission (1992b) *Getting the Act Together. Provision for Pupils with Special Educational Needs*. London: HMSO.

Audit Commission (1993) *Adding up the Sums: Schools' Management of Their Finances*. London: HMSO.

Audit Commission (1994) *Seen but Not Heard: Co-ordinating Community Child Health and Social Services for Children in Need*. London: HMSO.

Audit Commission (1996) *Misspent Youth . . . Young People and Crime*. London: Audit Commission.

Audit Commission (1998) *Misspent Youth 1998: The Challenge of Youth Justice*. London: Audit Commission.

Barrow, G. (1998) *Disaffection and Inclusion: Merton's Mainstream Approach to Difficult Behaviour*. Bristol: Centre for Studies on Inclusive Education.

Barton, L. and Tomlinson, S. (eds) (1981) *Special Education: Policy, Practice and Social Issues*. London: Harper and Row.

Becher, T. (1989) *Academic Tribes and Territories*. Milton Keynes: Open University Press.

Becher, T. (ed.) (1994) *Governments and Professional Education*. Buckingham: SRHE/ Open University Press.

Beek, C. (2002) The distribution of resources to support inclusive learning, *Support for Learning*, 17(1): 9–14.

Beveridge Report (1942) *Social Insurance and Allied Services*. Cmnd 6404. London: HMSO.

Bines, H. (1992) Interprofessionalism, in H. Bines and D. Watson (eds) *Developing Professional Education*. Buckingham: SRHE/Open University Press.

Bines, H. and Watson, D. (eds) (1992) *Developing Professional Education*. Buckingham: SRHE/Open University Press.

Birkett, D. (2001) The school I'd like, *Guardian Education*, 16 January.

Bishop, R. (2001) Designing for special educational needs in mainstream schools, *Support for Learning*, 16(2): 56–63.

Bowman, C. (1990) *The Essence of Strategic Management*. London: Prentice Hall.

Boyden, J. and Hudson, A. (1985) *Children: Rights and Responsibilities*. London: Minority Rights Group.

Bradshaw, J. (2001) *Poverty: the Outcomes for Children*. London: Family Policy Studies/National Children's Bureau.

Brink, B. (1997) *Guidelines for the Design of Centres for Street Children: Educational Buildings and Equipment*. Paris: UNESCO.

Broad, B., Hayes, R. and Rushforth, C. (2001) *Kith and Kin: Kinship Care for Vulnerable Young People*. London: National Children's Bureau.

Bronfenbrenner, U. (1970) *Two Worlds of Childhood: US and USSR*. New York: Sage.

Brooks, I. and Bate, P. (1994) The problems of effecting change within the British Civil Service: a cultural perspective, *British Journal of Management*, 5: 177–90.

Butler-Sloss, Rt Hon. Justice E. (1988) *Report of the Inquiry into Child Abuse in Cleveland 1987*. Cmnd 412. London: HMSO.

Cade, L. and Caffyn, R. (1994) The King Edward VI family: an example of clustering in Nottinghamshire, *Support for Learning*, 9(2): 83–8.

Campbell, D., Coldicott, T. and Kinsella, K. (1994) *Systemic Work with Organizations: A New Model for Managers and Change Agents*. London: Karnac.

Campbell, D., Draper, R. and Huffington, C. (1989) *A Systemic Approach to Consultation*. London: Karnac.

Chambers, R. (1997) *Whose Reality Counts: Putting the First Last*. London: Intermediate Technology Publications.

City of Edinburgh Council (1997) *Working Together: A Joint Report by the Directors of Education and Social Work*. Edinburgh: City of Edinburgh Council.

Clarke, M. and Stewart, J. (1997) *Handling the Wicked Issues: A Challenge for Government*. Birmingham: University of Birmingham Institute of Local Government Studies.

Clough, P. and Barton, L. (eds) (1995) *Making Difficulties: Research and the Construction of SEN*. London: Paul Chapman Publishing.

Cohen, R. and Long, G. (1998) Children and anti-poverty strategies, *Children and Society*, 12(2): 73–85.

Coleman, J. C. (1993) Understanding adolescence today: a review, *Children and Society*, 7(2): 137–47.

Coopers and Lybrand (1996) *The SEN Initiative: Managing Budgets for Pupils with Special Educational Needs*. London: Coopers and Lybrand for SEO/CIPFA.

Court Report (1976) *Fit for the Future: The Report of the Committee on Child Health Services*. Cmnd 6684. London: Department of Health and Social Services.

Davie, R., Upton, G. and Varma, V. P. (1996) *The Voice of the Child: A Handbook for Professionals*. London: Falmer.

DES (1965) *Circular 10/65: The Organisation of Secondary Education*. London: HMSO, 12 July.

DfE (1992) *Exclusions: A Discussion Document*. London: HMSO.

DfE (1994a) *Circulars 8–13/94: Pupils with Problems*. London: DfE.

DfE (1994b) *Code of Practice on the Identification and Assessment of Special Educational Needs*. London: DfE.

DfEE (1997) *Excellence for All Children: Meeting Special Educational Needs*. London: HMSO.
DfEE (1998) *Meeting Special Educational Needs: A Programme of Action*. Sudbury: DfEE.
DfEE (2001) *Diploma for Connexions Advisors: Introduction to Connexions*. Annesley: DfEE.
DfES (2001a) *Connexions for all: Working to Provide a Service for all Young People*. Annesley: DfES.
DfES (2001b) *Inclusive School Design*. Building Bulletin 94. Norwich: Stationery Office.
DfES (2001c) *Special Educational Needs Code of Practice*. Annesley: DfES.
DfES (2002) *Schools for the Future: Designs for Learning Communities*. Building Bulletin 95. Norwich: Stationery Office.
DoH (1989) *Introduction to the Children Act*. London: HMSO.
DoH (1998a) *Our Healthier Nation: A Contract for Health* (Green Paper). London: DoH.
DoH (1998b) *Working Together to Safeguard Children: New Government Proposals for Inter-agency Co-operation*. Wetherby: Department of Health.
DoH, DES and Welsh Office (1991) *Working Together: A Guide to Arrangements for Inter-agency Co-operation for the Protection of Children from Abuse*. London: HMSO.
DoH, DfEE and Home Office (2000) *Framework for the Assessment of Children in Need and Their Families*. London: HMSO.
Dorfman, A. (1997) *Widows*. London: Nick Hern.
Elton Report (1989) *Discipline in Schools*. London: Department of Education and Science and the Welsh Office.
Evans, J., Castle, F. and Cullen, M. A. (2001) *Fair Funding? LEA Policies and Methods for Funding Additional and Special Needs – and Schools' Responses*. Slough: NFER.
Exeter Youth Support Team (1992) A model of juvenile liaison. Unpublished paper, Exeter Youth Support Team, Exeter.
Fenichel, E. S. and Eggbeer, L. (1990) *Preparing Practitioners to Work with Infants, Toddlers, and Their Families: Issues and Recommendations for the Professions*. Arlington, VA: National Centre for Clinical Infant Programs.
Fish Report (1985) *Educational Opportunities for All? The Report of the Committee Reviewing Provision to Meet Special Educational Needs*. London: Inner London Education Authority.
Fletcher-Campbell, F. (1997) *The Education of Children Who Are Looked-After*. Slough: NFER.
Freeman, M. (1987) Taking children's rights seriously, *Children and Society*, 1(4): 299–319.
Fullan, M. G. (1992) Visions that blind, *Educational Leadership*, 49(5): 19–20.
Gardner, H. (1993) *The Unschooled Mind*. London: Fontana.
Gewirtz, S., Ball, S. J. and Bowe, R. (1995) *Markets, Choice and Equity in Education*. Buckingham: Open University Press.
Gill, K. and Pickles, T. (eds) (1989) *Active Collaboration: Joint Practice and Youth Strategies*. Glasgow: Intermediate Treatment Resource Centre.
Gillborn, D. (2001) 'Raising standards' or rationing education? Racism and social justice in policy and practice, *Support for Learning*, 16(3): 105–11.
Gillborn, D. and Youdell, D. (2000) *Rationing Education: Policy Practice and Equity*. Buckingham: Open University Press.
Gleick, J. (1988) *Chaos*. London: Cardinal.
Glenny, G. (2000) *Thame Children and Young Persons' Inter-agency Network: Evaluation of Projects Funded by the Calouste Gulbenkian Foundation*. Oxford: Oxford Brookes University, School of Education.
Glenny, G. (2001) *Hamilton Oxford Schools Partnership (HOSP): Integrated Support Services Evaluation Report*. Oxford: Oxford Brookes University, School of Education.

Graham, J. and Bowling, B. (1995) *Young People and Crime*. Home Office Research Study 145. London: HMSO.

Gray, P. (2001) *Developing Support for More Inclusive Schooling: A Review of the Role of SEN Support Services in English LEAs*. London: DfEE/NASEN.

Gray, P. and Dessent, T. (1993) Getting our act together, *British Journal of Special Education*, 20(1): 9–11.

Gulaboff, D. (1989) The MARS project in Dundee, in K. Gill and T. Pickles (eds) *Active Collaboration: Joint Practice and Youth Strategies*. Glasgow: Intermediate Treatment Resource Centre.

Gyarmati, G. (1986) The teaching of the professions: an interdisciplinary approach, *Higher Education Review*, 18(2): 33–43.

Hagen, U. and Tibbitts, F. (1994) The Norwegian case: child-centred policy in action?, in *The Politics of Linking Schools and Social Services: The 1993 Yearbook of the Politics of Education Association*. London: Falmer.

Hall, P. (1976) *Reforming the Welfare: The Politics of Change in the Personal Social Services*. London: Heinemann.

Hallett, C. and Birchall, E. (1992) *Co-ordination and Child Protection: A Review of the Literature*. Edinburgh: HMSO.

Hambleton, R., Essex, S., Mills, L. and Razzaque K. (1995) *The Collaborative Council: A Study of Inter-agency Working in Practice*. London: LGC Communications.

Hancox, L. (1999) Child Impact Statements: an experiment in childproofing legislation, *Young Minds*, 41: 9.

Handy, C. (1985) *Understanding Organisations*, 3rd edn. Harmondsworth: Penguin.

Hart, S. (1996) *Beyond Special Needs: Enhancing Children's Learning through Innovative Thinking*. London: Paul Chapman Publishing.

Herbert, E. (1998) Included from the start? Managing early years settings for all, in P. Clough (ed.) *Managing Inclusive Education*. London: Paul Chapman Publishing.

Hertfordshire County Council (2001) Children, schools and families, *Inform*, March: 25.

Hey, A. (1979) 'Organising teams – alternative patterns, in M. Marshall, M. Preston Shoot and E. Winnicott (eds) *Teamwork – For and Against*. Birmingham: BASW.

Higgins P. M. and Jaques, D. (1986) Training for teamwork in health care, *Higher Education Review*, 18(2): 5–19.

Hodgkin, R. and Newell, P. (1996) *Effective Government Structures for Children: Report of a Gulbenkian Foundation Inquiry*. London: Calouste Gulbenkian Foundation.

Holtermann, S. (1996) The impact of public expenditure and fiscal policies on Britain's children and young people, *Children and Society*, 10(1): 3–13.

Home Office (1962) *Non-Residential Treatment of Offenders Under 21*. London: HMSO.

Home Office (1965) *The Child, the Family and the Young Offender*. Cmnd 2742. London: HMSO.

Hornby, S. (1993) *Collaborative Care: Interprofessional, Inter-agency, Interpersonal*. Oxford: Blackwell.

Huffington, C. and Brunning, H. (1994) *Internal Consultancy in the Public Sector: Case Studies*. London: Karnac.

Hutton, W. (1995) *The State We're In*. London: Jonathan Cape.

Huxham, C. (1996) Advantage or inertia? Making collaboration work, in R. Paton, G. Clarke, J. Lewis and P. Quintas (eds) *The New Management Reader*. London: Sage.

Huxham, C. and Macdonald, D. (1992) Introducing collaborative advantage: achieving inter-organizational effectiveness through meta-strategy, *Management Decision*, 30(3): 50–6.

Huxham, C. and Vangen, S. (1996) Working together: key themes in the management of relationships between public and non profit organisations. Paper prepared for the

International Research Symposium on Public Services Management, 'Public Services in the Next Millennium: Working Together or Falling Apart', Aston Business School, March.

Hyams-Parish, A. (1996) *Banished to the Exclusion Zone.* Colchester: The Children's Legal Centre.

Include (2000) *This Time I'll Stay.* Ely: Include.

Jaques, D. (1986) *Training for Teamwork: Report of the Thamesmead Interdisciplinary Project.* Oxford: EMU/Oxford Polytechnic.

Johnson, D., Ransom, E., Packwood, T., Bowden, K. and Kogan, M. (1980) *Secondary Schools and the Welfare Network.* London: Allen & Unwin.

Jones, R. and Kerslake, A. (1979) *Intermediate Treatment and Social Work.* London: Heinemann.

Kadel, S. and Routh, D. (1994) Implementing collaborative services: new challenges for practitioners and experts in reform, in *The Politics of Linking Schools and Social Services: The 1993 Yearbook of the Politics of Education Association.* London: Falmer.

Kahn, A. (2002) Monitoring provision for pupils with special educational needs in Norfolk LEA: evaluation of effectiveness, *Support for Learning,* 17(1): 15–18.

Kanter, R. M. (1984) *The Change Masters.* London: Unwin.

Kempson, E. (1996) *Life on a Low Income.* York: Joseph Rowntree Foundation.

Kendrick, A. and Fraser, S. (1993) *A Study of the Integration of Child Care Services in Scottish Social Work Departments. Report on Stage 1.* Dundee: Department of Social Work, University of Dundee.

Kendrick, A., Simpson, M. and Mapstone, E. (1996) *Getting It Together. Changing Services for Children and Young People in Difficulty.* York: Joseph Rowntree Foundation.

Kilbrandon Report (1964) *The Report of the Committee on Children and Young Persons in Scotland.* Cmnd 2306. Edinburgh: HMSO.

Kingdon, D. G. (1992) Interprofessional collaboration in mental health, *Journal of Interprofessional Care,* 6(2): 141–7.

Kirst, M. W. (1991) Improving children's services: overcoming barriers, creating new opportunities, *Phi Delta Kappan,* 72(8): 615–18.

Knapp, M. S., Barnard, K., Brandon, R. N. *et al.* (1994) University-based preparation for collaborative interprofessional practice, in *The Politics of Linking Schools and Social Services: The 1993 Yearbook of the Politics of Education.* London: Falmer.

Kosko, B. (1993) *Fuzzy Thinking.* London: HarperCollins.

Kumar, V. (1993) *Poverty and Inequality in the UK: The Effects on Children.* London: National Children's Bureau.

Kurtz, Z., Thornes, R. and Wolkind, S. (1994) *Services for the Mental Health of Children and Young People in England: A National Review.* London: Department of Public Health, South Thames RHA.

Lacey, P. (2001) *Support Partnerships: Collaboration in Action.* London: David Fulton.

Lacey, P. and Lomas, J. (1993) *Support Services and the Curriculum.* London: David Fulton.

Lackoff, G. and Johnson, M. (1981) *Metaphors We Live By.* Chicago: University of Chicago Press.

Lee, S. (1986) *Law and Morals: Warnock, Gillick and Beyond.* Oxford: Oxford University Press.

Leeson, P. (1989) Open and inter-active learning: the LAP Programme, in N. Jones and T. Southgate (eds) *The Management of Special Needs in Ordinary Schools.* London: Routledge.

Lewis, A. and Lindsay, G. (eds) (2000) *Researching Children's Perspectives.* Buckingham: Open University Press.

Lewis, J. and Utting, D. (2001) Made to measure? Evaluating community initiatives for children: introduction, *Children and Society,* 15(1): 1–4.

Little, V. and Tomlinson, J. (1993) 'Education: thirty years change – for better for worse?, *Children and Society*, 7(2): 148–63.

Lloyd, C. (1993) *Rowntree Project. Young People in Difficulties: Research Findings*. Oxford: Oxford Council for Voluntary Action.

Lloyd, C. (1994) *The Welfare Network: How Well Does the Net Work?* Oxford: Oxford Brookes University, School of Education.

Lloyd, C. (1998) Inter-agency training in social work practice. Unpublished MA dissertation, Oxford Brookes University, School of Education.

Lloyd, G., Stead, J. and Kendrick, A. (2001) *'Hanging On in There': A Study of Inter-Agency work to Prevent School Exclusion in Three Local Authorities*. London: National Children's Bureau/Joseph Rowntree Foundation.

Lothian Regional Council (1991) *Report on the Work of School Liaison Groups: Session 1990/91*. Edinburgh: Lothian Regional Council, October.

Lothian Regional Council (1992) *Youth Strategy: Guidelines for School Liaison Groups*. Edinburgh: Lothian Regional Council, January.

Lovey, J., Docking, J. and Evans, R. (1993) *Exclusion from School: Provision for Disaffection in Key Stage 4*. London: David Fulton/Roehampon Institute.

Lunt, I., Evans, J., Norwich, B. and Wedell, K. (1994) *Working Together: Inter-school Collaboration for Special Needs*. London: David Fulton.

McCabe, A., Lowndes, V. and Skelcher, C. (1997) *Partnerships and Networks: An Evaluation and Development Manual*. York: Joseph Rowntree Foundation.

Maginnis, E. (1989) Lothian Region's youth strategy: a political perspective, in K. Gill and T. Pickles (eds) *Active Collaboration: Joint Practice and Youth Strategies*. Glasgow: Intermediate Treatment Resource Centre.

Mapstone, E. (1983) *Crossing the Boundaries: New Directions in the Mental Health Services for Children and Young People in Scotland*. Edinburgh: HMSO.

Marshall, S. and Elliott, J. (2001) Personal advisers to students in schools: practice and implications. Paper presented at the British Educational Research Association Annual Conference, Leeds, September.

Martin, C. (1997) *The ISTD Handbook of Community Programmes for Young and Juvenile Offenders*. Winchester: Waterside Press.

Mattessich, P. and Monsey, B. (1992) *Collaboration: What Makes It Work?* St Paul, MN: Amherst H. Wilder Foundation.

Mawhinney, H. B. (1994) Discovering shared values: ecological models to support interagency collaboration, in *The Politics of Linking Schools and Social Services: The 1993 Yearbook of the Politics of Education Association*. London: Falmer.

Meijer, C. (ed.) (1999) *Financing of Special Needs Education: A Seventeen-Country Study of the Relationship Between Financing of Special Needs Education and Inclusion*. Middelfart: European Agency for Development in Special Needs Education.

Mid Glamorgan Social Crime Prevention Unit (*c*.1992) *Crime, Alcohol, Drugs and Leisure: A Survey of 13,437 Young People at School in Mid Glamorgan*. Bridgend: Mid Glamorgan Social Crime Prevention Unit.

Midwinter, E. (1977) The professional-lay relationship: a Victorian legacy, *Journal of Child Psychiatry*, 18: 101–13.

Mitchell, D. E. and Scott, L. D. (1994) Professional and institutional perspectives on interagency collaboration, in *The Politics of Linking Schools and Social Services: The 1993 Yearbook of the Politics of Education Association*. London: Falmer.

Mort, V. (1999) Control, empowerment and change in the work of voluntry organisations: an ethnographic study of agencies working with single homeless people in Oxford. Unpublished Doctoral thesis, Oxford Brookes University, School of Planning.

Moss, P. and Petrie, P. (1997) *Children's Services: Time for a New Approach*. London: Institute of Education, University of London.

Muir, L. (1984) Teamwork, in M. R. Olsen (ed.) *Social Work and Mental Health*. London: Tavistock.

National Association for Remedial Education (1979) *The Role of Remedial Teachers: Guidelines No. 2*. Stafford: NARE.

National Foundation for Educational Research (1997) *Current Practice for Resourcing Additional Educational Needs in Local Education Authorities*. Slough: NFER.

National Union of Teachers (1984) *Corporal Punishment: The Case for the Alternatives*, 2nd edn. London: Education Department, National Union of Teachers.

Newell, P. (1988) Children's rights after Cleveland, *Children and Society*, 2(3): 199–206.

Newell, P. (2000) *Taking Children Seriously: A Proposal for a Children's Rights Commissioner*. London: Calouste Gulbenkian Foundation.

Nind, M. and Hewett, D. (1994) *Access to Communication: Developing the Basics of Communication with People with Severe Learning Difficulties through Intensive Interaction*. London: David Fulton.

OCVA (1991) *First Report of the Inter-agency Working Party on Children and Young People in Difficulty*. Oxford: Oxford Council for Voluntary Action.

Ofsted (1993) *Exclusions: A Response to the DfE Discussion Paper*. London: HMSO.

O'Neill, O. (1986) *Faces of Hunger: An Essay on Poverty, Justice and Development*. London: Allen & Unwin.

Organisation for Economic Co-operation and Development/Centre for Educational Research and Innovation (1995) *Children and Youth at Risk*. Paris: OECD.

Owen, H. (1996) *Creating Top Flight Teams*. London: Kogan Page.

Oxfordshire Health Authority (1995) *Report of the Inquiry into the Circumstances Leading to the Death of Jonathan Newby*. Oxford: OHA.

Parsloe, P. (1981) *Social Services Area Teams*. London: Allen & Unwin.

Parsons, C., with Benns, L., Hailes, J. and Howlett, K. (1994) *Excluding Primary School Children*. London: Family Policy Studies Centre.

Payne, M. (1982) *Working in Teams*. Birmingham: BASW.

Payne, L. (2002) Children's rights and impact analysis: making children visible in government, *Support for Learning*, 17(3): 127–31.

Pilkington, E. (1993) Community care begins at home, *Search*, 17 September, 5–7.

Plowden Report (1967) *Children and Their Primary Schools*. Central Advisory Council for Education (England). London: HMSO.

Roaf, C. (1999a) Funding SEN in mainstream schools: establishing a mechanism for Oxfordshire. Unpublished report for Oxfordshire Local Education Authority.

Roaf, C. (1999b) Appendices Q, R, T and V in Networks for Support: factors contributing to successful inter-agency work with young people. Unpublished Doctoral thesis, Oxford Brookes University, School of Education.

Roaf, C. (2001) Working with outside agencies, in J. Wearmouth (ed.) *Special Educational Provision in the Context of Inclusion: Policy and Practice in Schools*. London: David Fulton/The Open University.

Roaf, C. and Bines, H. (1989) *Needs, Rights and Opportunities*. London: Falmer.

Roaf, C. and Lloyd, C. (1995) Multi-agency work with young people in difficulty, in *Social Care Research Findings No. 68*. York: Joseph Rowntree Foundation.

Ruskin, J. (1867) *Time and Tide, by Weare and Tyne*, (1994 edition). London: Routledge/Thoemmes Press.

Rutter, M. (1980) *Changing Youth in a Changing Society: Patterns of Adolescent Development and Disorder*. Cambridge, MA: Harvard University Press.

Sampson, O. C. (1980) *Child Guidance: Its History, Provenance and Future*. London: British Psychological Society, Division of Educational and Child Psychology.

Seebohm Report (1968) *The Report of the Committee on Local Authority and Allied Personal Social Services*. Cmnd 3703. London: HMSO.

Seebohm, F. (1989) *Seebohm Twenty Years On: Three Stages in the Development of the Personal Social Services*. London: Policy Studies Institute.

Senge, P. (1999) *The Dance of Change: The Challenge of Sustaining Momentum in Learning Organizations*. London: Nicholas Brealey.

Sereny, G. (1995) *The Case of Mary Bell: A Portrait of a Child who Murdered*. London: Pimlico.

Social Information Systems (1993) *New Approaches to Managing and Monitoring Children's Services under the Children Act*. Knutsford: SIS Ltd.

Solity, J. and Bickler, G. (1994) *Support Services: Issues for Education, Health and Social Services Professionals*. London: Cassell.

Stone, M. (1981) *The Education of the Black Child in Britain*. Glasgow: Fontana.

Surrey County Council (1992) *Youth Link*. Woking: Woking Youth Office.

Swadener, B. B. and Lubeck, S. (eds) (1995) *Children and Families 'at Promise'*. Albany: State University of New York.

Swann Report (1985) *Education for All. The Report of the Committee of Inquiry into the Education of Children from Ethnic Minority Groups*. Cmnd 9453. London: Department of Education and Science.

Taylor, M. (1981) *Caught Between: A Review of Research into the Education of Pupils of West Indian Origin*. Windsor: NFER/Nelson.

Thomas, G. (1992) *Effective Classroom Teamwork: Support or Intrusion?* London: Routledge.

Thomas, G. and Loxley, A. (2001) *Deconstructing Special Education and Constructing Inclusion*. Buckingham: Open University Press.

Tomlinson, S. (1982) *A Sociology of Special Education*. London: Routledge and Kegan Paul.

University of North London Truancy Unit, Truancy Research Project (1994) *Truancy in English Secondary Schools: A Report for the DfE by the Truancy Research Project, 1991–1992*. London: HMSO.

Utting Report (1991) *Children in the Public Care*. London: Department of Health/Social Services Inspectorate.

Vagg, J. (1987) *Support for Difficult to Place People in Oxford*. Oxford: The Elmore Committee.

Warnock, M. (1998) *An Intelligent Person's Guide to Ethics*. London: Duckworth.

Warnock Report (1978) *Special Educational Needs: Report of the Committee of Enquiry into the Education of Handicapped Children and Young People*. Cmnd 7212. London: Department of Education and Science.

Weatherley, R. and Lipsky, M. (1977) Street level bureaucrats and institutional innovation: implementing special education reform, *Harvard Education Review*, 47(2): 171–97.

Webb, A. (1982) Strained relations, *Social Work Today*, 13(42): 10–11.

Welton, J. (1985) Schools and a multi-professional approach to welfare, in P. Ribbins (ed.) *Schooling and Welfare*. Lewes: Falmer.

Welton, J. (1989) Incrementalism to catastrophe theory: policy for children with special education needs, in C. Roaf and H. Bines (eds) *Needs, Rights and Opportunities*. London: Falmer.

Wilson, A. and Charlton, K. (1997) *Making Partnerships Work: A Practical Guide for the Public, Private, Voluntary and Community Sectors*. York: Joseph Rowntree Foundation.

Wright, H. J. (1980) The widening gyre (II), in O. C. Sampson (ed.) *Child Guidance: Its History, Provenance and Future*. London: British Psychological Society, Division of Educational and Child Psychology.

Index

DECONSTRUCTING SPECIAL EDUCATION AND CONSTRUCTING INCLUSION

Gary Thomas and Andrew Loxley

Deconstructing Special Education and Constructing Inclusion is a sophisticated, multidisciplinary critique of special education that leaves virtually no intellectual stone unturned. It is a must read for anyone interested in the role and significance of inclusive pedagogy in the new struggle for an inclusive society.

Professor Tom Skrtic, University of Kansas

In this book the authors look behind special education to its supposed intellectual foundations. They find a knowledge jumble constructed of bits and pieces from Piagetian, psychoanalytic, psychometric and behavioural theoretical models. They examine the consequences of these models' influence for professional and popular thinking about learning difficulty. In turn, they explore and critique the results of this dominance for our views about children who are different and for the development of special education and its associated professions. In the light of this critique, they suggest that much of the 'knowledge' of special education is misconceived, and they proceed to advance a powerful rationale for inclusion out of ideas about stakeholding, social justice and human rights. Concluding that inclusion owes more to political theory than to psychology or sociology, the authors suggest that a rethink is needed about the ways in which we come by educational knowledge. This is important reading for students of education, and for teachers, advisers and educational psychologists.

Contents
Special education: theory and theory talk – The knowledge-roots of special education – The great problem of 'need': a case study in children who don't behave – Thinking about learning failure, especially in reading – Modelling difference – Inclusive schools in an inclusive society? Policy, politics and paradox – Constructing inclusion – References – Index.

160pp   0 335 20448 1 (Paperback)   0 335 20449 X (Hardback)

INCLUDING PARENTS?
EDUCATION, CITIZENSHIP AND PARENTAL AGENCY

Carol Vincent

- How do parents and professionals experience their involvement with locally-based education groups?
- Who joins local groups and who gets involved in campaigns?
- What do their experiences of 'including' themselves tell us about public participation and citizenship today?

Carol Vincent focuses upon the neglected topic of lay activity in relation to education. She describes the experiences and motivations of parents involved in a variety of grass-roots groups, organizing around educational issues, and examines their problems and successes. She explores how parents' relationships with educational institutions cast light on the broader issues of public participation and how citizenship is experienced today by different social class and ethnic groups.

Contents

Parents and education: consumers, partners or citizens? – Being a 'good' parent – Seeking advice: the special education advice centre (SEAC) – Education for motherhood? – Parents, collective action and education – An alienating system? – Conclusion – Including parents? – References – Index.

176pp   0 335 20442 2 (Paperback)   0 335 20443 0 (Hardback)

SPECIAL EDUCATIONAL NEEDS, INCLUSION AND DIVERSITY: A TEXTBOOK

Norah Frederickson and Tony Cline

This book has the potential to become *the* textbook on special educational needs. Written specifically with the requirements of student teachers, trainee educational psychologists, SENCOs and SEN Specialist Teachers in mind, it provides a comprehensive and detailed discussion of the major issues in special education. Whilst recognizing the complex and difficult nature of many special educational needs, the authors place a firm emphasis on inclusion and suggest practical strategies enabling professionals to maximize inclusion at the same time as recognizing and supporting diversity.

Key features:

- takes full account of linguistic, cultural and ethnic diversity unlike many other texts in the field
- addresses the new SEN Code of Practice and is completely up to date
- recognizes current concerns over literacy and numeracy and devotes two chapters to these areas of need
- offers comprehensive and detailed coverage of major issues in special educational needs in one volume
- accessibly written with the needs of the student and practitioner in mind.

Contents
Part 1: Principles and concepts – Children, families, schools and the wider community: an integrated approach – Concepts of special educational needs – Inclusion – Special educational needs: understanding pathways of development – Part 2: Assessment in context – Identification and assessment – Reducing bias in methods of assessment – Curriculum-based assessment – Learning environments – Part 3: Areas of need – Learning difficulties – Language – Literacy – Mathematics – Hearing impairment – Emotional and behavioural difficulties – Social skills – References – Index.

528pp   0 335 20402 3 (Paperback)   0 335 20973 4 (Hardback)